"I have been a fan of Maribeth Ekey for a long time. Now, she presents her wisdom in this wonderful book that will prevent much dread and sorrow. If you are plagued by unfulfilled wishes, Maribeth has hope for you."

STEPHEN ARTERBURN
Co-founder and Chairman, New Life Ministries

"Sometimes when we wish and dream, we lose. What to do then is always a problem. Dr. Ekey gives us guidance on redeeming our losses so we can dream, and live, again."

HENRY CLOUD, PH.D.
Author of *Changes that Heal* and co-author of *Boundaries*

"We all struggle with knowing when to open ourselves up to wishing and hoping, and when it is time to accept reality and let go. Dr. Ekey has written an extremely helpful book on understanding how to wish. I recommend it to those struggling with losses as well as anyone involved in the personal growth journey."

JOHN TOWNSEND, PH.D.
Author of *Hiding from Love* and co-author of *The Mom Factor*

"Learning to mourn and let go of the idealized, wished for (but non-existent) spouse and *love the real person* is at the core of what makes marriages thrive. With poignant illustrations, Dr. Ekey describes how to mourn the loss of the ideal so you can love the real. We heartily recommend *Shattered Hopes, Renewed Hearts* to those struggling with disappointment in marriages...and to those struggling with any profound disappointment that they just can't seem to shake."

DENNIS DEL VALLE, L.M.F.T. and
KIMBER DEL VALLE, PSY.D.
Del Valle Relational Institute

"*Shattered Hopes, Renewed Hearts* is a must-read for anyone who has struggled with unmet wishes. With winsome, wise story-telling, Dr. Ekey helps us discern between helpful and harmful wishing. Artfully she teaches us how to get past those unrealistic wishes we bring to people, careers, and even to God...so that we can know the joy of wishes that do come true."

AARON J. REINICKE, L.M.F.T. and
MELINDA REINICKE, PSY.D.,
Author of *Parables for Personal Growth*
Reinicke Counseling Associates

SHATTERED HOPES, RENEWED HEARTS

What to Do with Wishes That Don't Come True

Maribeth Ekey, Psy.D.

Foreword by Paul Meier, M.D.

WESTBOW
PRESS®
A DIVISION OF THOMAS NELSON
& ZONDERVAN

WestBow Press books may be ordered through booksellers or by contacting:

WestBow Press
A Division of Thomas Nelson & Zondervan
1663 Liberty Drive
Bloomington, IN 47403
www.westbowpress.com
1 (866) 928-1240

Scripture quotations taken from the New American Standard Bible® (NASB), Copyright © 1960, 1962, 1963, 1968, 1971, 1972, 1973, 1975, 1977, 1995 by The Lockman Foundation Used by permission. www.Lockman.org

ISBN: 978-1-9736-5974-7 (sc)
ISBN: 978-1-9736-5976-1 (hc)
ISBN: 978-1-9736-5975-4 (e)

Library of Congress Control Number: 2019904184

Print information available on the last page.

WestBow Press rev. date: 5/30/2019

To my daughters,
Mekdes and Zinash,
two amazing young ladies
who have lived out the wisdom in this book
with such grace and courage;

And in memory of their Ethiopian parents,
Alemayehu and Tsegie
who loved them so well during their young formative years
and raised them to have a rare wisdom,
capacity for love, kindness and resilience.

You were well-loved then, and you are so loved now.

CONTENTS

SECTION 3
WISHING, MOURNING, AND JOY

SECTION 4
UNIVERSAL WISHES WE NEED TO LET
GO OF IN ORDER TO KNOW JOY

FOREWORD

As a psychiatrist, I help many people regain joy in their lives by supporting them in giving up on idealistic fantasies that will never come true while at the same time encouraging them to have a positive and realistic vision for their own future. The Bible says that where there is no vision, the people perish; so having attainable dreams is an important part of life. In her book, Dr. Maribeth Ekey, with whom I cohosted radio programs for years, has done an excellent job of helping us to see the difference between a vibrant, hopeful vision for the future and dead-ended, unrealistic fantasies that only create bitterness and depression. She helps us understand how these haunting unrealistic fantasies come into being in the first place, and how to work through them to the freedom to passionately pursue wishes and dreams that can come true.

The book is a celebration of our courage to stretch ourselves beyond ourselves and go for what we truly want in life—and of the joy that can come as we creatively make our wishes and dreams come true. It is also a celebration of the God who grants us our deepest desires—and the courage, wisdom, and resources to pursue them.

But the same wishing that so enriches our lives also can leave us vulnerable to hurt or sadness at times. Nights of weeping *do* happen, and we need to know how to face and transform such nights into the promised shouts of joy (Ps 30). Dr. Ekey gives hope, meaning, and dignity to the mourning process as she vividly illustrates—by telling stories as well as by teaching specific steps—how people get through their disappointed wishes to a greater sense of wholeness, freedom, and aliveness. One sees that there is, indeed, life after loss; and although no one is always happy, joy honestly can be the bottom line of our lives.

I highly recommend this book to anyone who wants to experience personal growth, added joy, and renewed motivation and energy to fulfill their goals for the future.

—Paul Meier, M.D.

ACKNOWLEDGMENTS

I am so very grateful to the people who have loved and supported me in this project.

Thanks to Phil Sutherland and Althea Horner who, in their day, contributed so meaningfully to the discipline of psychology (their contributions live on) and did so much to help me and countless others face and mourn our unrealistic wishes that we might live fully and wholly.

Thanks to the Institute of Spiritual Formation (ISF) at Talbot (Biola University in La Mirada, California), whose students have taught me so much about pushing through shattered hopes to relentlessly pursue growth in their Christian faith.

Thanks to Betsy Barber (Associate Director of ISF), a dear friend whose deep faith encourages and informs my own, along with her husband, Steve Barber.

Thanks to Penny Hansen, a wise, gently incisive spiritual director who invited me into a fuller, more joyous knowledge of the treasure that is ours through faith in Christ.

Thanks to my women's group, including Kimber Del Valle, Sharon Lewis-Bultsma, Lisa Rowley, Mary Manix, and Trang Leete (excellent psychologists all), who challenge my thinking, keep me honest and sharp, and are so very fun to celebrate life with.

Thanks to John Carter and Linda Barnhurst and Thomas and Evelyn Okamoto, cherished friends whose stimulating conversations have inspired countless useful insights about Christianity and psychology.

Thanks to WestbowPress Editorial for their fine editing along with Jessica Snell, Mark Cerbone, Daniel Peckham, and Betty Talbert for their valuable editorial and/or design input.

Thanks to Maureen Price, prized friend and coworker who gave the gracious final nudge that got this book back into print.

Thanks to John Townsend and Henry Cloud, whose professional support has been invaluable and unstinting and whose friendship is a pleasure.

Thanks to Steve Arterburn, who has been generous in his kind words and support and in the rewarding professional opportunities he has created for so many of us.

Thanks to Paul Meier, one of the humblest and wisest men I've known who made doing radio such a pleasure.

Thanks to Melinda and Aaron Reinicke, my very dear friends who have enriched my life with their love and have always rooted wholeheartedly for my life wishes;

Thanks to David and Denice Ekey, warm, generous family who have been tirelessly committed to helping family and friends realize our deepest wishes;

Thanks to Jim and Cyndi Telander, Roger and Laura Conover, Richard and Marge Avery, Rob and Robin Brennan, David Hendrick and Stephanie Nigh, Nikki Grimes, the Elisaras and the Wards, Sallie and dear Nefsie. These longtime friends *are* wishes come true and have been the source of so much wisdom, warmth, and laughter.

SECTION 1

ALL ABOUT WISHING

CHAPTER 1

THE LOST ART OF WISHING

Two beloved Jewish ancestors, Hannah and Abraham, had something in common—a wish. They both wished fervently for a son. Both diligently pursued their wishes, even in the face of disheartening obstacles, including being misunderstood by those close to them. And both experienced their wishes coming true. The fulfillment of their wishes—the birth of their sons—changed the course of history.

A dear friend of mine, Melinda, had it easier than Hannah and Abraham. With little worrying and waiting and without dramatic bargaining with God, she had two darling boys. She cherished and enjoyed her boys, and she felt deeply grateful for the added richness and pleasure they brought to her life.

While they adored their boys, Melinda and her husband, Aaron, longed deeply for a little girl. However, they encountered difficulty getting pregnant a third time. And after a while, Melinda began to face the strong possibility she would not have her own little girl.

At this point, Melinda confronted a choice. On the one hand, she could hang on to her wish to give birth to her own little girl through various behaviors, such as

- becoming consumed with arduous strategies to bring about the wanted pregnancy as she had less and less time and energy for her husband and sons;
- secretly resenting her youngest son for not being a girl or resenting her husband for not producing that second X chromosome (blaming others is a subtle way of hanging on to our wishes); or,
- allowing her grief to become a lasting monument to her wishes for a daughter, settling into a bitterness that blocked her joy and creativity in life.

Melinda made a different choice. She began to mourn and let go of her wishes for the third pregnancy and the possibility of a daughter. With great sadness, she thought about the many things she would never experience with a daughter—mother-daughter banquets, playing with dolls together, and those first dabbles with makeup. She confronted and let go of her fantasies of dress shopping with her little girl and teaching her to shop cleverly for bargains. Reluctantly, she realized she would never get to enter into a young teen's wrestling with the art of womanhood. Nor would she get to teach her daughter how winsomely strength and beauty can flow together in femininity.

She wept as she reflected on these experiences she longed to share with her daughter. She genuinely loved her husband and sons and the life they had together, but she felt deeply sad as she let go of the strong desire that was not materializing. Even so, she did not let herself get lost in or overwhelmed by her sadness.

As she mourned and honestly faced her life without a little girl of her own, her longings gradually shifted and took a new direction. An idea came to her—the idea of adopting a baby girl from an Asian orphanage. Aaron agreed wholeheartedly with her idea. They soon began the long, tedious, and expensive process of adoption. There were many setbacks in the adoption process, but Melinda and Aaron persevered. As Melinda dreamed of and looked forward to her adopted baby girl, she described her joy as similar to what she experienced when pregnant with her boys.

How did Melinda face the disappointment of her original wish? She confronted her deep longings, mourned them, and formed them into a new plan. As a result, a little baby girl was chosen out of a faraway orphanage and invited into a remarkable existence of love, warmth, and opportunity that she could never have dreamed of. The course of one child's life was changed dramatically by my friend's wish. (And I had the inestimable privilege of being with Melinda and Aaron as they met their baby girl for the first time.)

Big Outcomes

We, too, need to wish—and wish fervently. Our wishes can impact the world. Our wishes motivate us and channel and focus our life energy and passion. They make the difference between merely plodding through a day or feeling fully alive and invested in this task we call living. When we wish, we look forward. We hope and strive with a sense of meaning.

Our wishes can also stretch us and help us grow in unexpected ways. We have all felt inspired by accounts of people who have overcome great odds, such as David defeating Goliath…or Joni Eareckson Tada and Christopher Reeve triumphing over quadriplegia…or Alex Honnold accomplishing the first free solo climb of the sheer granite cliff of El Capitan…or people of faith persevering through harsh persecution to a refining and strengthening of their faith.

Or perhaps you know something about the history of Beethoven. A homely bachelor, he was often intensely in love yet not loved in return. He was going deaf and given to bouts of deep depression. Struggling with a death wish in a despairing letter to his brothers in 1802, he decided he did not want to die before he had composed all the music he could. Beethoven was facing and working through his many disappointed longings in favor of a still deeper passion— his desire to express his musical gift. The immediate result was his magnificent *Third Symphony,* which changed musical history. Before he died, Beethoven composed his famous *Ninth Symphony,* a rousing celebration of our ability to transform deep sorrow into joy.[1]

These people have made and are making an impact on the world by making wishes and dreams come true.

The magic in these real-life stories is that they encourage us to wish and dream. Big outcomes can start with simple wishes, wishes we want badly enough to push beyond ourselves in our effort to realize them. As we push further than we ever thought we could, we transcend ourselves. We uncover unfathomed depths and untapped strength in ourselves. We achieve outcomes we'd hardly dared to believe possible.

Life's Curveballs

We all face the kind of crossroads and choices Melinda faced at some time in our lives. We all know what it is to wish fervently and then have life throw us a curveball that leaves us with deep disappointment. For one person, the curveball may be a spouse who is not available in ways one had hoped. For another, it's rejection by someone who seemed to be the love of his or her life. Perhaps such a disappointment may involve physical setbacks, such as heart disease or cancer. Or it may involve the serious illness of a child or the loss of closeness with a child who has become strangely distant. For someone else, it may be the unexpected loss of a rewarding and lucrative career. Whatever the particular loss we experience, we all have had wishes that seemed within our grasp suddenly slip away. And many of us know what it is to go on doggedly and desperately pursuing a wish long after it has proven impossible.

In the face of life's curveballs, it is helpful to understand why we hang on to unrealistic wishes too long and how to let go of them so we can pursue wishes in line with reality. When we do, we can experience the joy of wishes that *do* come true.

The Art of Wishing

There is an art to wishing the way my friend Melinda and other triumphant people have wished. Their triumphs have not come easily, for wishing involves passion and risk. It involves letting ourselves deeply want something, and we are never more vulnerable than when we deeply want something. It also involves letting our passions propel us into unknown territory—a risky, unsettling experience. The art of wishing challenges us to discern what is *real* so that we can recognize when to let go of and mourn unrealistic wishes and then let our passions take us in another direction.

We all know that art is different from formula. It is more intuitive, less clear-cut. But if a formula can be applied to the kind of wishing Melinda did, it has three elements—wishing, mourning, and joy. Melinda's story models for us a triumphant way to approach our wishes. We can wish deeply, mourn the loss of our wishes when they prove unrealistic, and free our passions to invest in wishes that *can* come true so that we can know joy.

Clearly, the ability to wish and the ability to mourn unfulfilled wishes are in tension with each other. But if we are to wish well, we need to do both—wishing and mourning—even though they seem almost mutually exclusive.

First, we wish passionately. A woman yearns for her husband to stop abusing her and to treat her with dignity and tenderness. A person struggles to launch a career as an artist, attorney, or psychologist. A single person centers his or her whole life around the search for a mate. Such wishes motivate us and make us determined and wholehearted in our pursuit of them.

Second, we remain open to mourning the loss of our wishes. This is where the tension mounts. Even as we persistently pursue our wishes, we remain attentive to reality. When reality tells us persistently the wish is not going to happen, we are wise to give it up. After we have tried many angles to achieve our wishes, there comes a time to mourn and let go of them.

Third, our mourning eventually leads us to greater freedom, wholeness, and joy. But the actual process is painful. The abused wife faces her intense wish that her husband were kinder, more loving, less self-absorbed, and less raging, while she also faces the simple reality that he is who he is. As she does this, she feels deeply sad. That sadness enables her to let go of her unrealistic wishes and act realistically toward him. She begins to learn how to set effective limits on his abuse rather than to wish passively for him to change.

The would-be attorney needs to face his deep longings to be a high-powered criminal lawyer. Ever since his college days, he has dreamed of reforming the legal system. While letting himself feel the full brunt of these longings, he must also address certain realities. He feels impotent in his three-year struggle to establish himself, and he cannot live on loans and his wife's salary forever. Meanwhile, his seventy-hour workweeks are costing him precious time with his young sons. As he makes himself look at all aspects of reality, his inner longings actually change. He feels deep sadness about what is not happening in his legal career, and that sadness actually shifts his desires and efforts. He is freed up to pursue realistic goals.

In mourning the loss of their wishes for marriage, single persons must face their longings for closeness, for the prestige of being one of a pair, for the comfortableness of that built-in community, and for the specialness of feeling chosen and cherished. Even as they acknowledge these deep yearnings, they also make themselves accept the fact that they *are* single. They then feel the sadness of their unrealized dreams in a way that enables them to let go of the "marriage-around-the-corner" fantasy and live life fully as they are right this moment. It is not that they will never marry. It is that they get a new settledness in who they are right now. They are freed up to simply live *life*—not married life or single life but *life* itself.

Tolerating the Tension

Often, at the point of experiencing the tension of wishing intently but not knowing if we will get what we want, we run aground. If we could wish and be certain our wish would come true, it wouldn't be so difficult. Or it may seem more tenable to simply quit wishing so that we never have to risk not getting something in which we are so invested. But to wish and not know if our wish will be realized can certainly seem unbearable.

So we try to step out of this tension. We may do what a man named Bill did. He strongly wished for a certain woman to respond to his intense passion for her. Bill wanted this woman's affection so badly that he wouldn't let himself face the possibility she might have no interest in him. He launched a rigorous spiritual regimen of prayer, fasting, and Bible study to assure himself that God would make this relationship happen. A close friend, who saw and understood what Bill was doing, confronted him about trying to manipulate God *and* the woman. He suggested that Bill give the relationship the time every relationship needs to unfold and simply wait to see if their relationship would work. If over time the woman wasn't interested in him, Bill shouldn't ask God to reorganize this woman's whole being into someone who could like him. After all, the friend continued, *liking* this woman meant Bill should respect her and the choices she makes. In time, if she didn't appear interested, Bill would clearly need to mourn and let go of unrealistic wishes toward her. With reluctance, Bill heard his friend's wise words. In time, he observed the woman's clear lack of romantic interest and then began a very sad process of letting go. This became a sobering time of self-exploration to try to understand why he had so wanted to possess and change another human being.

Like Bill, often we try to step out of the painful tension of not knowing whether we will get the things we truly want, and we do this in a variety of ways. We try to escape the uncertainty of wishing by

- assuring ourselves that God has promised us our desired outcome, perhaps thinking, *God gave me that verse for this very situation*;
- being so good that we think we deserve the fulfillment of the wish, secretly presuming, *Not even God would dare turn down such virtue*;
- serving others sacrificially, subtly insisting, *Surely someday someone will notice and start giving back to me*; or
- somehow trying to coerce others into giving us what we want, with an implied, *See what a rough life I've had. You wouldn't want to add to the misery, would you?*

But the reality is that none of us has absolute control over whether or not our wishes come true or the assurance that they will. In James 4:13–16, God is very clear about our limitations in knowing and controlling the future. The best any of us can say is, "If the Lord wills, we shall live and also do this or that" (v. 15). Jesus modeled this subordinance to God's will in the garden of Gethsemane when he wanted something very badly—perhaps to avoid the agony of the cross—and said, in the middle of intense struggles, "Not My will, but Thine be done" (Lk 22:42).

God is sovereign; we are not. None of us has a guarantee our wishes will come true. If we are to wish well, we must pursue our desires wholeheartedly even while we are not certain of the outcome. We ask, we seek, and we knock (see Mt 7:7). We learn the joy of seeing our efforts bear fruit when our wishes come true. We can also experience an unexpected joy as we learn to mourn and let go of wishes that don't come true. In the process, we can also learn to trust God's will—and his very presence—as being far better for our lives than the particular wishes we had imagined.

Recapturing the Lost Art of Wishing

Our wishes and dreams—those things for which we yearn earnestly and deeply—are pivotal to living fully and to fulfilling our unique destiny in life. Our wishes provide focus, motivation, and *oomph* for our goals and pursuits. They also give us a sense of aliveness, vibrancy, and looking toward tomorrow. In fact, they go hand in hand with hope. Without our wishes and dreams, life would be flat and hollow.

But many of us have forgotten how to wish effectively. Somewhere along the way, we became afraid of the risks involved and traded in our wishes for secure outcomes. Or we began searching for a lamp and a genie that could guarantee us our outlandish wishes rather than allowing our wishes to propel us into the unknown. Or maybe because we were afraid that our wishes would degenerate into lustful desire, we cowered in a seemingly righteous apathy. And some of us, in order to protect ourselves, quit wishing and adopted the sure formula that said, "If I really don't want anything, I can't be disappointed."

It is imperative that we recapture the lost art of wishing, for only then can we become people who, inspired by our passions, can accomplish the great works of our forebears, including

- Abraham and Hannah, who each had a deep, relentless longing to have a son;
- the apostle Paul, whose life was set on fire by a fervent desire to be with Christ; and
- that dreamer Joseph, whose dreams propelled him into an uncanny world, so unexpected but so necessary.

This book is dedicated to teaching the lost art of wishing. It provides a map for discovering our own soul's wishes and ways to teach our children to discover theirs. It outlines a plan for pursuing our goals and dreams wholeheartedly. It warns us to discern when wishes prove unrealistic. It teaches us how to listen to our unrealistic wishes and to understand what they are telling us about our past.

And last, it shows a way to muster the great courage needed to mourn and let go of unrealistic wishes so we can be involved—fully and passionately—in a real world with real people where wishes really do come true.

CHAPTER 2

THE CHILD'S WORLD OF WISHING

Lou Gehrig is a name almost everyone has heard. For a long time, he held the record for the most consecutive baseball games played—2,130 of them! In the summer of 1995, Cal Ripkin Jr. broke Lou Gehrig's record. An interview with Cal Ripkin shortly after he entered the record books illustrates a key point: We all need the passion of our wishes to motivate us in pursuing our goals.

Asked how he felt about sharing this record with Lou Gehrig, Ripkin said it wasn't just holding the record that he had in common with Lou Gehrig. Of greater significance was the passion and motivation they shared. The record had been merely a side effect of the endless practice motivated by their passion for baseball and for excellence.

This passion and the extraordinary discipline it required didn't start when Cal Ripkin was in his twenties. I imagine it started when he was a child growing up in a family that was willing to listen to and encourage him to follow his heart's desires.

As with little Cal Ripkin, so it is with all children. Our wishes— even at a young age—are very important. Our earliest wishes and desires provide the singular source of motivation for the arduous task of living out God's unique will in our lives. Hopefully, we begin discerning our destiny in early childhood, when, through wise education given by our parents, we learn who we are and what unique desires and talents we were created to express.

Born to Wish

When we are babies, we already know how to wish because we are born a *nephesh*—a living soul. In Hebrew, the word *nephesh* refers to the seat of our desires.[1] Babies and young children have within them the soul skill of wishing, yearning, and longing. It comes naturally to them. The apostle Peter even uses babies as a model for how we are to yearn (in this case, for the Word of God): "like newborn babes, long for the pure milk of the word" (1 Pt 2:2). Babies do not need instruction in how to wish. They already know.

But babies do need a lot of help in fulfilling their wishes, and this is where parents come in handy. Initially, a child is absolutely dependent on the parent for getting what he or she *wants* or *wishes* in life. The child is also dependent on the parents for his or her *needs*—that which is necessary for survival, such as food, water, warmth, and physical contact.

Sometimes, as we grow older, however, it becomes easier for us to give more credence to our *needs* than to our *wishes*. It seems more right or justified to meet our needs. Indeed, the growing child must learn that it is right to honor needs over wishes at times.

But wishing is also good. It is vital to our well-being. And as parents honor their babies' wishes and wants, the babies sense that wishing is good and keep on wishing.

Wishing and Wisdom

The parent brings wisdom—maturity, experience, and mastery of the world—to the child's wishes. At first, according to the developmental needs of the infant, the parent simply tries to figure out what the infant is wanting and then meets his or her wishes.

Not long ago, an infant named Sarah nestled in her mother's arms while I was talking intently with the woman about a business project. Without warning, the mother's attention shifted from our business to Sarah. She held Sarah up in the air, playing with her, and cooed, "Do you want attention?" Apparently, this mother had heard the "I want attention" cry from her infant. I had been absorbed in our business discussion and had not gotten the message. But this mother's ear was trained to hear her infant's heart wishes. She heard and responded.

Baby Sarah learned two very important lessons from this interaction. First, she learned that it was safe to want. She would not be shamed or punished for wanting. Sarah's mother communicated, "Your wants are welcome here!" by responding to her infant so warmly and naturally. This is a very important message. One day when God tries to communicate this same message to little Sarah, she will be able to understand more readily because of this early training from her mother.

Second, Sarah learned what her specific wish was. Obviously, at this young age, Sarah didn't understand her mother's words, so she did not think, *Oh, it's attention I'm wanting!* It would be quite some time before Sarah could translate her wishes into words. But her mother's *actions* have begun to communicate to Sarah what it is that Sarah herself wants. In this instance, Sarah sensed at this preverbal age that something was wrong. Then when Mommy played with her, she suddenly felt much better. Through this wordless gratification, Sarah began to learn that closeness with Mommy brings fulfillment of her intense longings. (How nice for Sarah that her first wishes can afford to be wishes for closeness with another person!)

Like Sarah, all infants need to have their minds read and their wishes granted by a fairly indulgent mother or father. But eventually, the emerging toddler needs to be weaned from this instant gratification unless one wants to create a totally spoiled child.

Mourning the loss of our wishes starts early in life! Gradually, the parents reduce indulgence and teach the growing children how to satisfy their wishes on their own. For children to learn how to fulfill their own wishes, three things need to happen.

First, children need to know what their wishes are. The parents' task is to teach their children to know their own *nephesh* (soul), and that knowledge includes knowing what they truly want in life. The parents must teach the developing children to put their wishes into words and then to take responsibility for pursuing those core wishes and desires. When correctly translated, Proverbs 22:6 says, "Train up a child in his proper way and when he is old he will not depart from it."[2] This verse supports what psychologists have learned: parents need to discern children's desires, wishes, talents, natural bents, and preferences and then train these children to know and pursue their own desires and talents. This aspect of parenting is crucial to children's well-being. When children's goals flow from an accurate channeling of their core desires and talents, they are likely to stay on course for the rest of their lives.

Second, parents need to teach their children how to pursue their wishes wisely. This wisdom includes knowing how to delay gratification, apply disciplined effort, fail gracefully, master setbacks, persevere, and tolerate deprivation. This wisdom also includes balancing personal wishes and wants with the wishes and wants of others. This calls for finesse in creating win-win situations for everyone involved so that children are not always getting their wishes at other people's expense. (Wishes gained at other people's expense result in a loneliness that isn't anybody's idea of a wish come true, and children need to learn this.) As children work to apply the skills of wisdom to their wishes, they learn the truth of Ecclesiastes 5:3, which says, "For the dream comes through much effort…"

Third, parents need to teach their children wisdom for knowing when to let go of wishes. Wisdom says there is a time to mourn (see Eccl 3:4), and children need help in discerning when this time has come. A daughter might need her parent's tender instruction to understand that even though she prayed and prayed, the puppy is not going to get better. Or maybe a son has worked and worked at mastering soccer. He wants desperately to be able to play with his older sister but just doesn't have the coordination yet. He needs his father to lead him away from soccer and help him get excited about something he *can* do.

When children mourn the loss of their unrealistic wishes, they need comfort from their parents. A child's wishes need to be taken very seriously. At the core of most of our losses is the disappointment of unfulfilled wishes. Our losses don't just involve people who have left or puppies that have died. Our losses also involve the now impossible wishes and dreams that might have been realized with the people or puppies that are no longer in our lives. It is comfort that makes the difference between a loss that is overwhelming and a loss that is manageable.

Children need to know their losses are real, their sadness is normal, and it won't last forever. They need to be taught there is life after disappointed wishes, and they need to be helped to reengage in life.

The Missing Piece…and How Children Lose Touch with Their Wishes In Shel Silverstein's book for children called *The Missing Piece*,[3] a Pacman-like creature (a circle with a triangle portion missing) rolls through life looking for the perfect piece to fill in its hole. The creature rolls bumpily along, trying to fit different objects into its missing piece. It tries various circular and oblong pieces until it finds the perfect fit (which turns out to be not so perfect after all).

This creature's search for a missing piece provides an apt analogy for what goes wrong in the upbringing of many children and why many of us became adults who are off-center and don't know our *nephesh*, our core desires. After all, like Shel Silverstein's creature, every human being has missing pieces. The fact that we sin and have been sinned against guarantees that we have missing pieces or brokenness. We tend to try to use other people to fill in our holes.

We often do this automatically and without calculation, and we are especially prone to use other people to fill in our holes if we haven't done the soul-searching necessary to identify what our core desires are. When it comes to filling holes in our lives, we are quickest to use those closest to us…or those who need us.

Thus, parents often unwittingly use their children to fill up their holes. When children are used as objects for fulfilling parents' unmet wishes, the children have a difficult time knowing the wishes and desires of their own souls. What happens is that the children are not known in their own right by their parents. Therefore, they cannot know themselves well. Rather bits and pieces of the children's souls—and at times, huge, glaring portions of them—are shaped to fit the children into the parents' missing pieces.

This fit soothes the parents and creates a connection between the parents and children. Children desperately need a connection with their parents, and therefore, they are masters at discerning what they need to do in order to secure it. This connection with their parents is the children's number-one wish *and* their most important psychological need. But the cost is great when children must fit their parents' missing pieces in order to be connected. Children's souls then become reflections of their parents' missing pieces rather than the unique reflection of God's image that they were intended to be. In this process, children get cut off from their own desires and wishes.

Consider a little boy who simply longs for warm hugs from his parents but has a macho father who shames the child's longings. Not surprisingly, the child learns to swagger through little boyhood—and manhood—as though he didn't want hugs at all. Or perhaps a little girl dreams about being an Olympic ice skater and demonstrates some genuine talent to back the dream. But her highly intellectual and mathematical mother cannot get excited about ice skating. So the little girl leaves her skates behind and gets *excited* about her multiplication tables.

Or think about what happens when a retiring, hesitant mother always hushes her gregarious and highly amusing son. He stays gregarious and amusing, but there is a certain hollowness to the fun. (Where would we be if Johnny Carson had had such an upbringing?)

Each of these examples illustrates how children can lose touch with the longings and yearnings of their own souls. Souls aren't usually lost in dramatic, one-time events. They are more often lost in the subtle, day-in, day-out interactions between parents and children in which parents simply don't hear and thereby squelch the soul wishes of their children.

Losing touch with our soul wishes proves a major problem throughout life. When we pursue goals, we must be able to tolerate frustration, setbacks, and deprivation. Pursuing goals requires a lot of motivation, and our core desires and wishes are what provide this motivation. They are the source of energy with which we pursue goals and live life well. When we find ourselves faking our desires or trying to live out someone else's desires (like a parent's), our motivation tends to run dry. We feel we are running on empty. We're not really empty, but we've cut the fuel line to our own energy source—the desires of our own *nephesh*.

Our Task as Adults

As parents, none of us can reflect perfectly our children's souls. We see through a mirror dimly (see 1 Cor 13:12). The static of our own wishes and needs necessarily interferes with the clarity of our perceptions of who our children really are. Inevitably, we miss knowing them, and we fail to help them get to know parts of themselves. This is a tale that has been retold and reaffirmed from the time of Adam and Eve to the present day. Sins and distortions have been passed from parents to children from the beginning. All of us are sinners. All of us come from and produce dysfunctional or sinful families.

As adults, we all face life with portions of our soul wishes unknown or blotted out. Our task as adults, then, is to search out our own souls, to get to know ourselves, to discover our deepest wishes and longings, and to figure out how to pursue them. This, in fact, is what maturity or adulthood is—taking responsibility for our own souls. And a crucial aspect of taking responsibility for our souls is clarifying our own soul wishes.

CHAPTER 3

THE ADULT'S WORLD OF WISHING

We all have wishes that begin in childhood. However, in the process of growing up, our wishes may become muddled. Then when we are grown, we often find ourselves intently pursuing wishes and goals we cannot have. The pursuit of unattainable wishes makes us miserable. Furthermore, the adult's real wishes and needs are paralyzed by unresolved longings from childhood. To resolve the dilemma posed by these muddled wishes, we need to sort the child's wishes from the adult's wishes. We have to learn to distinguish between our true soul wishes and the wishes of our parents, whom we tried to please. We need to face and mourn the disappointed wishes of childhood so we can stop being caught up in fruitless pursuit of them. We must hang on to the child's fervent wishing while balancing it with the adult's wisdom, discernment, and love for others in pursuing our deepest wishes.

That's what Nickie discovered. Nickie had been married for seven years to a solid, reliable, and at times adventurous man who loved her. Many of her girlfriends envied her, and she knew it. But she did not have romantic feelings toward him. Both he and their relationship felt stale, bland, and disappointing to her. She struggled with a profound sense of, *Is this all there is?*

Without realizing it, Nickie and her marriage were being driven by an unstated wish from childhood that centered around unfulfilled longings for her mother. Nickie had adored her mother, but her mother had been absorbed in her husband. She had little time or patience for Nickie's pestering, and secretly, she regretted the distraction from her husband that Nickie caused her. Recognizing her own feelings and limitations, she wisely refrained from having any more children. So Nickie was left longing intensely for a mother who would at least go through the motions of mothering. Sometimes when a mother is unavailable in this way, a daughter will go to her father with her longings, but Nickie's father stayed absorbed in his work in a way that left him unavailable to her as well.

Nickie was in a bind, and as children often do, she *wished* her way out of the bind. From childhood on, she imagined a fantasy solution to her problem. It went like this: "If I can find an ideal man out there, then I can kill two birds with one stone. I can impress Mom, who seems to get really absorbed in ideal men, and I can replace Dad." (Wishes are not usually this clearly stated, but they can become clear if we honestly look at what we are pursuing in life.)

Nickie knew what her mom liked in men, so she set out to capture this *ideal* man. Of course, there are no ideal men, and those who did appear ideal to Nickie were not capable of real intimacy. But Nickie went on pursuing this wish because doing so gave her hope for finally getting what she had always wanted from her mother.

Her hope, however, was bought at a high price. Eventually, because she wanted children, Nickie married Jay. Unlike the men she was always pursuing, Jay *was* capable of commitment and love. But he left her mother cold. Marrying Jay did not bring Nickie any special acknowledgment from her mother. So Jay wasn't the man of her dreams. He couldn't be since her wishes still centered around unmet longings for her mother. The result was that Nickie always had a vague sense that Jay was distracting her from what she truly wanted in life, and she was unable to love and enjoy her husband.

If Nickie were to work through this dilemma, she would have to face her unresolved yearnings from childhood. She would have to mourn and let go of the wishes and unfulfilled longings of her childhood in order to be able to figure out what and who she really wanted in life. She would need to confront her own past and her own soul in order to free herself to live fully and wholly as an adult.

As adults, we all face Nickie's dilemma. In a nutshell, the task of taking responsibility for our own souls and our own soul wishes (to be examined in depth in the chapters ahead) takes the following steps:

Step 1: Confront the sad side of life.

Usually, as in Nickie's case, we don't confront the sad side of life. It confronts *us*. We can go a long time pretending that sadness and badness don't exist, that they are anomalies or exceptions to the rule of our lives. We can pretend that if we do the right things, we can avoid sadness. But then something happens that overwhelms our ability to manipulate and control life, and suddenly, there we are, trying to deal with staggering sadness.

In Nickie's case, she had put hard, concentrated effort into pursuing her version of an ideal life in which she had a mother who loved her in the ways she had always wished. In Nickie's mind, when she attained this wish, she would have secured for herself a happily-ever-after future. It was a perfect plan. But her life had not followed the plan. She felt listless and disengaged as she pursued her wish.

It is good when sadness confronts us because it helps us give up the wish for a pain-free, ideal life. Often we start pursuing a wish for a pain-free life when childhood losses, sadness, and fears seem too great and when there is no one to comfort us and help us make sense of it all.

Children don't know what to do with their losses. So they try to ignore them and enter a fantasy world in which things are magically *all better*. At any hint of pain, they begin to automatically withdraw into that seemingly safe place where they hope to escape the hurtful realities of life.

When we've become adults, we may well continue the child's search for a pain-free reality, a sad-free happiness, and a guaranteed love without loss. But life is not pain-free, and our quest for pure happiness is an unrealistic wish for things to be other than what they are. Children protect themselves with this defensive wish. But when adults try to live in a fantasy world, it will cost them dearly.

Our distorted wishes leave us dealing with the wrong problem. When sadness happens, we treat it as something that *should not have been*, and we redouble our efforts to create a pain-free life. In his book, *The Road Less Traveled*, Scott Peck writes, "Life is difficult."[1] Once you realize this truth, life ceases to be so difficult because now it is no longer an issue for you. It is like this with the sadness of life.

Once we accept that life is sad, once we stop fighting our sadness and simply let it be, we can channel our energies into facing sadness constructively. As we face it, we mourn. As we mourn, we let go of wishes and dreams that *cannot* be. In letting go, we free our passions for investment in wishes that *can* be. This is the road to joy.

One day we will live in a pain-free world. God will wipe the tears from our eyes, and there will be no more mourning (see Rv 21:4). But that is not the way things are now. Now life is painful and sad at times, and the cost of avoiding reality is greater than the cost of learning to accept reality. There is greater efficiency, creativity, and productivity when we invest our passions and energies in dealing with reality rather than in resisting it. There is greater wholeness—and therefore greater joy—when we stretch ourselves to embrace happiness *and* sadness rather than when we try to embrace happiness only.

*Step 2: Face our disappointed wishes of childhood
from an adult's vantage point.*

A wise psychologist named Phil Sutherland once said, "The goal of therapy is sadness." Can't you just see it in a Google ad?

"Phil Sutherland, Ph.D. MY GOAL IS YOUR SADNESS."

It would not make for great marketing. Most people come to therapy in hopes of becoming happy. But the goal of therapy *is* sadness. The goal is to lead those who are seeking help to face and work through the deep sadness at the core of their disappointed childhood wishes. The goal is to sort out past from present losses so individuals do not have to be terrified of past sadness. It really doesn't have the same power in adulthood that it had in childhood, unless we allow it power. Loss is a normal part of life, but when adults continue to struggle with unresolved losses from childhood, loss feels highly abnormal. The unresolved losses from childhood in addition to the normal losses of adulthood really do feel overwhelming and unbearable. The resolution is not to try to avoid further loss by walling ourselves off and deciding not to want anyone or anything in life. The resolution is to work through childhood losses so that we can be free to wish, want, and love as adults and also to embrace the normal (even "necessary"[2]) losses that go with this process. As we rework our childhood losses from an adult vantage point, we begin to see that loss is manageable after all. We can feel loss, and we don't have to avoid it at all costs.

That's what Nickie did. She began to explore why she wanted to detach from a real man like Jay. She found it was her own distorted way of wishing for her mother. She then began to explore past losses that involved both her mother and her father and that had been masked by her distorted wishes. That was the hard part. Looking at those past losses exposed her to feelings she had determined in a little girl's wisdom to *never* feel again. They had seemed too awful and overwhelming, but now she began to allow herself to experience her losses. As she delved into her memories, she remembered in vivid detail the many losses related to her parents, and she sobbed. She felt the child's inability—the sheer helplessness—to make Mom and Dad love her in the ways she so desperately wanted. There were times when these feelings were so intense she had difficulty functioning at her job. On occasion when driving she had to pull over to the side of the road because tears came too fast. She slept restlessly, sometimes hardly at all. Nickie was facing the original loss and sadness. She was mourning.

As she grieved, Nickie found that as an adult, she was stronger than the losses that had overwhelmed her as a child. To her surprise, she discovered that she had the power and resources to begin to embrace and integrate these memories and feelings. Somewhere along the line, reality had changed. The childhood feelings had not really been *so* big. It was just that the child had been so little.

There were other differences too. When she was a child, her family had been her whole world, and often they had been better at creating loss than at comforting it. But now her world was much bigger. Now she had some wise people who were willing to stand by her side and comfort her as she confronted her early losses. She had other resources she had not had as a child—more wisdom, more intelligence, better problem-solving skills, and an ability to discern reality that went far beyond simply accepting the myths that had been told her as a child.

Even with all these resources, she still had a difficult time facing and working through her disappointed wishes and the intense feelings that went with them. Sometimes Nickie found herself momentarily lost back in her childhood memories, feeling exactly how she had felt then—hopeless and terribly sad. But she had people in her corner who were gently and determinedly reminding her, "That was then. It was awful…and overwhelming. It shouldn't have happened. But that was long ago. Things can be different now." So Nickie drew from the strength and wisdom of adulthood as she worked at resolving the haunting losses of her past.

The result was that Nickie came to see herself very differently. She no longer saw herself as a child who'd been victimized by life. Instead she came to appreciate, believe in, and respect herself, her struggles, and her power to resolve those struggles. She even could understand the crazy predicaments that her efforts to protect herself had created. In all these realizations, she was embracing a bigger, more multifaceted self.

As she grew, her relationship with Jay also grew. She found she truly liked Jay and wanted to get to know him in his own right, not just as bait for attracting her mother. His straightforward, honest, and even unglamorous qualities held increasing appeal for her as she gained insight into herself and her past. Nickie was facing and letting go of her unrealistic wishes toward her mother that had caused her to have unrealistic wishes toward men. She was becoming free to enter into a loving and even romantic relationship with her husband.

Step 3: Let people know about your pain and
sadness so they can comfort you.

The presence of people in Nickie's corner who said, "It was awful… but that was then. Now can be different," was crucial in Nickie's coming to grips with her sadness. These people are comforters. Jesus's statement "Blessed are those who mourn, for they shall be comforted" (Mt 5:4) teaches us at least two things—that mourning can lie in the road to happiness and that comfort while mourning is pivotal to finding happiness. Whether our mourning involves reworking past losses or embracing the here-and-now losses and sadness that come from wanting things and people intensely, comfort is an essential part of coming to grips with our disappointed wishes.

Sometimes as would-be comforters, we distinguish between *real* losses and the losses that come from disappointed wishes and dreams. For example, sometimes we offer profuse comfort to the one whom we feel has experienced a *real* loss like death or divorce. But regarding the person who is finally letting go of highly unrealistic longings for a mother or the person who is finally getting out of a dead-end relationship that we knew all along was merely wishful thinking, we simply think, *It's about time!* and offer little comfort. But these losses we call *real* and the losses that come as a result of disappointed wishes are the same.

Disappointed wishes are at the core of all our losses, and there is no harder work in life than grieving the loss of our wishes as they prove unrealistic. We must have comfort when, even as adults, we are grieving the loss of our childhood wishes and dreams. As we mourn and let go of the child's wishes, we are freed up to search our own souls and to uncover the adult's wishes as Nickie did.

Step 4: Work to discover or uncover your soul's wishes through a process of soul-searching.

Nickie gradually transformed her childhood relationships and the wishes and longings that had been a part of them. The transformations took place as she gave new meanings to these past events and as she applied an adult's wisdom and understanding to the events. It may sound like Nickie was wallowing in her past. She was not. Rather she was productively working through her current feelings and perceptions regarding these past events. The process actually allowed her to experience her present life more fully. It also allowed her to experience wishes and dreams for her future—to know her own soul and its deepest longings and to pursue these longings unhampered by ghosts from her past. This is the purpose of mourning and letting go of our unrealistic wishes from childhood.

Searching the Soul

But how do we know our deepest wishes and dreams? How do we know what we truly want in life? To answer this very important question, we must engage in a process of *soul-searching*—of questioning, exploring, confronting, and discovering the wishes, thoughts, feelings, and intentions of our own souls.

Fearing that such a process will leave them hopelessly self-centered or egotistical, religious people often balk at this task of soul-searching. In his book *Ancient Secrets*, a devout Jewish rabbi, Levi Meier, teaches that the religious person must do the "holy inner work"[3] of intently searching his or her own soul. He is right. It is primarily religion that has taught us that we have a soul (see Gn 2:7), that our soul is valuable and precious (see Ps 139:13–16), and that we are responsible for our souls and accountable to God for them (see Ez 18:4; Mk 8:36, 37; Phil 2:12, 13). Religion also teaches us that God searches our souls (see Ps 139:1–6, 23, 24; Rom 8:26, 27) and that we, too, are to search our own souls (see Pss 51:6; 19:12–14; 2 Cor 13:5; 1 Cor 11:28; Gal 6:4).

Thus, a biblical understanding of the soul teaches us that we are weighty beings who do not have the luxury of taking ourselves for granted. We must deal with ourselves; we must examine our souls.

But what exactly is soul-searching? How do we do it? There are many different techniques for soul-searching that people have taught through the centuries. But to search our souls, we have to quiet down in order to listen to our hidden motives, desires, feelings, thoughts, and intentions. This seems simple enough, but it can actually be quite difficult because we have gone to a great deal of effort throughout our lives to blot out or muffle parts of our soul that confuse, frighten, or disturb us. What follows are concrete tips to guide the somewhat mysterious process of soul-searching.

First, it is important to have a wise guide in the process of soul-searching, such as a mentor, spiritual director, therapist, or mature and honest friend. For Nickie, her soul-searching was carried out in therapy. Her therapist served several functions. He held her accountable to regularly face and deal with those parts of herself that had always frightened her. He helped her have compassion for herself. He brought an outside perspective to the task so that Nickie could see parts of herself to which she had been blind, and he also helped Nickie remain balanced in her soul-searching so that the process did not degenerate into a despairing introspection or a morbid self-preoccupation.

Second, as we seek to get to know hidden desires, thoughts, and motives in our souls, it is important to do it from a grace-based, nonjudgmental stance. One of the Greek words for "judge," *krinō,* can mean either discern or condemn,[4] and there are many scriptures that are given to free us from relentless condemnation of our own souls (see 1 Cor 4:3; Rom 8:1, 33, 34; Jn 3:17, 18; 8:10,11; 16:8–11; Mt 7:1–5). As we drop judgment—or labeling ourselves as bad because of our thoughts and feelings—we are freed up to discern or honestly face our motives, feelings, and thoughts (the good, the bad, the ugly, the petty, and the noble). We can accept them as real parts of us. We can then come to understand what these motives, feelings, and thoughts are telling us about ourselves and ultimately resolve unwanted thoughts and feelings.

For example, Nickie had a recurrent daydream about leaving Jay for an idealized man. She had been appalled at this sinfully adulterous fantasy. She had repeatedly put it out of her mind. Indeed, such a fantasy could be acted on in sinful ways that would hurt those around her. Nickie might have an affair with such a man. Or she might get so caught up in her fantasy world that she would be emotionally unavailable to her husband.

But fantasies can also be explored in ways that help us to be more honest about ourselves, gain understanding of our hidden motives, and work through them to greater capacity for love without actually acting them out.

In the safety of therapy, Nickie began to explore this idealized man of her fantasies. She came to understand how precisely he reflected the kind of man her *mother* idealized. From this insight she began to see how much her desire for a man revolved around her desire for her mother, and oddly, she saw that this fantasy man who had so haunted her thoughts was not at all what *she* really wanted in a man. Out of this series of insights, she was able to confront the task of mourning and letting go of her mother and was eventually freed up to love Jay in new ways. Thus, a fantasy that Nickie had judged as inherently evil (even apart from *acting on* the fantasy), once explored, provided the very keys needed to resolve Nickie's problem. Her exploration of the fantasy turned out to be a process of confession and repentance that resulted in bringing hidden thoughts and fantasies captive to the throne of Christ (see 2 Cor 10:5). At last, Nickie was cleaning a deeply embedded log out of her own eye and could see others much more clearly (see Mt 7:3–5). She could finally see that the problem was not with Jay but with herself.

Third, in listening to our own souls, we must come to embrace their complexity, their mysterious unknowns, and the tension or struggles that go along with our many competing wishes—some of which seem very good and some of which seem very bad. If we are to honestly observe ourselves, we must come to accept opposite motives in ourselves such as love and hate, altruism and selfishness, envy and well-wishing. Ecclesiastes 3:1–8 may help give us permission to embrace these opposite strivings in ourselves. But we must seek to listen to all of ourselves, not just the more ideal or pleasant yearnings and thoughts. This is certainly what Nickie was doing in her therapy when she painfully acknowledged and shared with another human being the shameful fantasy.

Fourth, we must discern which wishes to pursue and which ones to let go of either because they are unrealistic or because they are wrong and would hurt us and those around us (see Gal 5:17–25; 1 Cor 10:6; 2 Cor 13:5). In Nickie's case, she made a choice not to pursue her immense wishes for an ideal fantasized man because she believed her wishes to be wrong. Instead she closely examined her fantasy, came to understand deeper wisdom and insight about herself (see Ps 51:6), and worked through the fantasy to a more romantic love for her husband. Her increased romantic love for Jay was very much in line with deeper wishes Nickie had always had to marry a man she deeply loved. She believed those wishes were right and good, and she pursued them with delight!

Daring to Wish

This business of searching our souls is essential to discerning our soul wishes and to living life fully. Soul-searching requires hard, concentrated effort. It is a process that will force us, like Nickie, to mourn and let go of many wishes along the way so that we might know the fulfillment of deeper wishes. It is an ongoing task, one we must confront throughout our lives. (Our wishes often change or take new forms as we mature and go through different life stages). It is a process to be carried out on our own before God and with the help of God and the help of friends (comforters).

The well-known poet Tennyson once said, "'Tis better to have loved and lost than never to have loved at all." Or we might say, "Better to have wished and lost than never to have wished at all."

The choice to live life passionately and to embrace the losses that inevitably come with wishing is a hard choice. We can choose to wish only as:

- we understand that sadness is a part of life,
- we attain the strength that comes through facing the child's losses and working through them to new meanings in our adult life, and
- we let comforters into our lives who can encourage us when we falter.

In this process, we mourn and let go of the child's unrealistic wishes. We feel deeply sad about things we wanted and didn't get in our childhood. But as we face our losses, we are freed up to begin investigating our adult souls. We assume adult responsibility for knowing and pursuing our own wishes in the context of community. Only then can we begin to sense and to know what we really want in life and the unique calling toward which our soul wishes prompt us.

Some people who are afraid of loss will withdraw from wishing for or deeply desiring anything that is not already easily within their grasp. I don't condemn those who choose to avoid the risks of wishing and wanting. Most of us are in that camp at times. However, this book is dedicated to those who, even in the midst of their settled routine, wonder from time to time, "What do I really want in life?" It is for those who seek to live passionately and are willing to deal with the losses that necessarily come from daring to wish.

SECTION 2

WISHES THAT WON'T COME TRUE… AND THE HIGH COST OF PURSUING THEM

CHAPTER 4

DEFENSIVE WISHING — PART 1: SPLITTING

David was a young child whose parents loved him dearly but were simply too busy to notice many of his antics and daring, little-boy conquests. But David intensely desired his parents to notice and admire him. In order to deal with his frustrated wishes for attention, David learned to retreat into a rich internal world of fantasy in which he was on stage or in front of a TV camera where he was loudly cheered by a wildly enthusiastic audience.

David's fantasies lifted his spirits markedly. They soothed the feelings of deep pain and shame he experienced when his most charming attempts to engage his parents failed. But his fantasy world cost him dearly. By the time he was six years old and entering first grade, he was so absorbed in his fantasies that he would act them out regularly in the classroom. He was always trying some new gimmick to draw attention to himself. His untiring efforts to be the center of attention alienated his peers and thus blocked the very thing he so ardently desired—positive attention.

David was in a bind. When he was three years of age, his wish for his parents to adore and revel in his childish shenanigans and new masteries of the world was perfectly normal. To him, his new skills and capabilities were truly astounding, and he longed for his parents to be astounded too. His longings were healthy and appropriate for his age, but his parents did not realize fully what David wanted. They were absorbed with mortgages, jobs, and financial pressures, and without meaning to, they often frustrated David's wishes. So David created a fantasy world in which his wishes could come true.

Like David, many of us as children created rich imaginative worlds to offset our disappointed wishes. The greatest of these wishes was to be connected to our parents. Whether the connection involved being adored, being cuddled, having parents *ooh* and *aah* as we toddle independently away, having our ideas admired, or some other type of closeness, we all longed for connection with our parents. But these wishes were not always fulfilled. When the lack of fulfillment was too glaring, we often resorted to secondary wishes in an effort to compensate for the disappointment of our primary wishes and longings. We constructed imaginary worlds in which we were known and lauded in the ways we wished to be.

These secondary wishes—and the imaginary worlds we constructed for them—took many shapes and forms. In David's case, he imagined himself to be the center of admiring attention. Some have imagined themselves rich and powerful in their efforts to overcome the stigma of poverty. Others have imagined themselves as an only child when they have felt lost in a crowd of siblings. Still others have imagined that an adoring cat or puppy was somehow a parent figure in order to compensate for not feeling special to their parents. But whatever the specific content of our secondary wishes, the underlying purpose is always to protect the person wishing from the pain of unfulfilled longings.

Secondary wishes are called *defensive wishes* because their function is protective. Our defensive wishes provide imaginary worlds to which we can retreat and find temporary healing—or at least some reprieve from the pain—when our number-one wish for closeness with our parents is disappointed. But there is a problem with these defensive wishes and imaginary worlds. They are not and never can become *real*. They are wishes that come to absorb our best passions and energies. They are wishes that protect us from painful reality for a time. But they are unrealistic, and they can never come true.

Nonetheless, we hang on to our wishes tenaciously. We feel we cannot afford to let go of them. We would have to face our pain and sadness—our disappointed wishes for closeness—if we let them go. The cost seems too great, so we ignore the cues that tell us our wishes are unrealistic. We pursue our defensive but impossible wishes blindly and earnestly. In this way, we set ourselves up for repeated disappointment, and the ongoing sorrow becomes far worse than the original sadness against which we were defending ourselves in the first place.

We just don't get it. We don't understand the high cost of pursuing unrealistic wishes, and so many times as adults we continue to pursue them. Our wishes then come to shape many of our most important adult choices.

Defensive wishing is indeed the force behind many of the foolish choices we see one another making. Think about the man who marries an alcoholic woman for the third time. Consider the person who again and again pursues get-rich-quick schemes and glamorous careers for which she is not qualified. Over and over she fails, but if she had settled for an ordinary career with a steady salary, she could have enjoyed success and real money. Or think about the woman who really wants to marry but who over and over becomes involved with *charmers* who cannot settle down. Each of these choices is driven by defensive wishes. We watch and puzzle over these choices that are so clearly out of line with reality. We aren't privy to the defensive wishes fueling the unwise choices. We don't understand the magnitude of pain the person will have to face in order to give up these unrealistic wishes.

If we are to be free to make wise choices stemming from realistic wishes and desires, we have to mourn and let go of our defensive wishes. And in order to let go, we must understand more deeply their nature and what they cost us. To do this, we must understand three types of defensive wishing—splitting, spoiling, and wishing for the ideal. It may be helpful to first consider the phenomenon called *splitting*.

Splitting is a process of wishing away parts of ourselves. Like most defensive wishing, splitting originates in childhood and is carried into adulthood. When children split, they protect themselves from their own feelings by pretending they are not feeling them. In this way, they can ward off feelings that may seem overwhelming, scary, or threatening. These feelings may include rage so intense that a young girl feels she could kill someone. Or a little boy may feel a sadness so deep that it seems as if he might cry until he drowns in his tears. Or perhaps there is a terror so vivid that a child might scream forever and ever. By splitting off the feelings and wishing them away, children come to believe they really don't have them. This saves the children from being overwhelmed by feelings when there is no one available to help them work through their emotions—when there is no one to comfort, soothe, and explain these feelings to them. Feelings really do overwhelm children when there is no one available to comfort them.

Zach's Hidden Memories

One man named Zach remembers choosing to split off his feelings. He says that as a little boy, he discovered a black hole in the universe into which he could tuck unpleasant feelings and events. When Zach was very young, his family, which was fleeing persecution, escaped from their native country in a clandestine and highly dangerous operation. Zach's previously secure childhood then became a nightmare. The escape was followed by a gradual realization that he was a citizen from *nowhere* and that he could never go home again.

Subsequently, he also faced a forced, long-term separation from his parents and spent many years in orphanages.

The discovery of a black hole in the universe was one of the great events of his childhood. He felt heady with relief and power as he tucked away his awful feelings and memories. He stashed away the terrifying events that had happened during the escape. He buried his love and longing for his parents, who could not be with him. He hid his rage at his abusive caretakers with whom he dared not express his anger.

By tucking away the terror of his orphan's world, Zach could do everything required of him quite stoically. His powers were limitless. He was adaptive to a fault and seemed like the model child. Facing life in a foreign country where he was ridiculed by other kids for speaking such a strange language, he even tucked away his native tongue and resolved never to speak another word of it.

Since this was also the language of the mother and father who had seemed to abandon him, his decision never to speak the language felt like he was saying, "Good riddance." So thoroughly did he tuck his language away—so real is this phenomenon called splitting—that as an adult, he could not speak one sentence in his native tongue.

Like Zach, many children get caught up in splitting. The choice to split is a protective choice. The child protects his soul from overwhelming feelings that seem as if they could tear him into a million pieces. Backed into a corner, children like Zach make desperate, unconscious choices to protect their terribly small and vulnerable souls from being blotted out by an overwhelming reality.

Children make such unconscious choices when they have no awareness of other options. They react reflexively in the same way one draws a hand back from a flame. These unconscious, reflexive choices may become habitual over time, but the children never know what their options are or even that they are choosing.

These choices are made for the sake of survival. But in the long run, our efforts to create a safer world through splitting cost us in at least two ways. First, splitting takes the energy required to pursue our wishes and live life fully and channels it into keeping our feelings out of our awareness. The result is that we are left with markedly less energy for living life. We are drained and become exhausted easily. Second, when we keep *some* feelings out of awareness, the unintended result is that we keep *all* feeling out of awareness. We are built with an all-or-nothing thermostat on our feelings, and the cost of turning down the temperature on certain scary feelings is a numbing of all feelings. This makes for a bland, flat life. We end up numbing our very souls.

The choice to split is not usually remembered as vividly as Zach remembers it. And even he had forgotten about the existence of the black hole in the universe until one night he dreamed about a myriad of black cats pouring out of the black doorway of an attic and threatening to overrun the house. Cats had always been repulsive to him. In therapy, as we considered that the cats might symbolize some repulsive part of himself, he suddenly remembered the black hole in the universe, and the awful memories he had hidden there began to emerge.

In this analysis of his inner world, Zach was letting go of his defensive wish of splitting. As he let go, he found himself mourning. Letting go of defensive wishes always involves mourning because it requires facing sad or painful feelings we have tried to pretend we weren't really feeling. As we work through the defensive wish, we face and embrace the feelings we once worked so hard to avoid. Eventually, we come to see that the feelings that seemed so overwhelming to us as children cannot really *kill* us. We see that we do not have to give up our souls in order to ward them off.

Further, as we face and work through the sadness, we come to experience joy. Even though Zach was terribly sad, he was able to celebrate the richness and depth of facing his buried feelings—the glittering, awe-inspiring, multicolored *stalactites* and *stalagmites* of the hidden caverns of his soul. Zach's healing was taking place in the context of therapy, and as he said after a particularly sad and weepy session, "It's astonishing and kind of exciting the places I go on this couch. I think I experience more of life and adventure here than I could flying around the world three times." Zach was experiencing the increased wholeness and joy that come as we mourn and let go of our defensive wishes and embrace more of our real selves and our real world.

CHAPTER 5

DEFENSIVE WISHING —
PART 2: SPOILING

Spoiling is another form of defensive wishing. Spoiling is a way of pretending that *good* is *bad*, so we will not wish or long for someone who may reject us.

It works like this. Whenever we meet people who seem as if they might be pleasurable to get to know, we automatically start demeaning those people, turning them into undesirables in order to avoid longing for relationships that may not happen. The unchallenged premise from childhood is as follows: "My wishes never come true. Therefore, I won't wish. Therefore, I must spoil whatever looks like it might be desirable." Our single-minded pursuit is to protect ourselves from unfulfilled longing. However, without realizing it, through the process of spoiling, we continually destroy any possibility for good in our lives. When we get through, we discover we have wished into existence a world more undesirable than the real world.

Consider the case of Brittany. Brittany had a macho father. Macho men are men who spoil—or demean—women. Reflexively, compulsively, and without understanding their own motives, macho men belittle and criticize women. Their hidden motives lie in a deep-seated fear of their own little-boy wishes for mother. Somewhere along the line, these men had their longings for mother shamed, so they started running from their longings. They began spoiling. As they grew up, *mother* for these macho men translated into women at large. They especially came to spoil those for whom they would otherwise long intensely. The more desirable the woman, the more intense the spoiling.

Brittany's mother was attractive, intelligent, sexy, and altogether desirable. That posed a problem for Brittany's father. He wanted his wife, but he didn't want to want her. He resolved his dilemma through spoiling. He frequently demeaned her by putting her down.

At three years of age—that glorious age when little girls fall head over heels in love with their daddies—Brittany faced an unstated but terribly compelling dilemma. She was in love with her father but still very dependent on her mother. She longed for her mother, while her father demeaned her mother. Confronted with this seemingly forced choice, Brittany chose her father over her mother.

It is tragic when children feel they have to choose between a mother and a father. It's also very tragic when a little girl chooses to erase from her life her mother and all the wonderful, necessary wishes and longings that are natural for a child to feel toward her mother. But this was Brittany's choice. In her little-girl adoration of her father, she allied with his spoiling. In the process, she squelched her longings for her mother.

The larger picture is that in the bargain, Brittany joined in with her father's spoiling of womanhood, including, of course, her own. She grew up to be a *macho woman*. In this role, she became a successful businesswoman and thoroughly enjoyed her career. She also enjoyed her dad's pride in her for being one of the guys. But there was a cost to her spoiling. She was so busy proving she was not a despicably weak woman that she could not be vulnerable enough in relationships to become close to men or women.

This is the result of spoiling a parent, especially a mother. The child's first and most intense relationship is with the mother. If the mother is spoiled—if the child works at framing the mother as bad in order to be protected from longing for her—the child is left with glaring holes in his or her heart and soul.

God warns us against dishonoring our parents, and he says that our well-being is linked to honoring them (see Eph 6:1–3; Ex 20:12). Defensively wishing away our parents through spoiling—making them less desirable than they really are—is the essence of dishonoring them, and it does indeed lead to emptiness rather than to well-being. It leads to emptiness in part because whenever we *spoil*, we also *split*. When we devalue another, we blot out parts of ourselves. This was certainly true in Brittany's case. She blotted out her own good feelings about being a woman as she mimicked her father's spoiling of her mother.

Spoiling also leads to emptiness because it kills off people in our inner world. Our inner world is filled with our feelings toward family, friends, and even enemies. It is our good feelings about these people and our good feelings about ourselves as we relate to these people that lead to a sense of fullness and well-being.

The resolution to our emptiness and lack of well-being, then, is to work through our defensive detachment from our parents and come to a point where we can evaluate realistically who they are and the impact—good or bad—they have had on our lives.

Brittany needed to give up defensively wishing away her mother. She needed to understand why she had devalued her and work through that issue so she could value her mother realistically. It was only as Brittany became more realistic in her love for her mother that she could become more realistic in her love for herself and her own womanhood. She also had to give up idealizing her father. (Idealizing or wishing for the ideal is covered in the next chapter.)

Five years ago Brittany bought a home by a charming brook. When the home was in escrow, she fantasized about having worship times while looking out over the lovely brook and forested area that formed the backyard. But the years went by, and as one year turned into another, she never sat on the patio to worship while viewing the lovely brook and forest. She never even furnished the patio. It remained empty just like the inner space in her heart where her mother should have been.

One spring day it suddenly occurred to Brittany that the patio had never been occupied. That day, for the first time, she *heard* the brook babbling and inviting her to worship God. She *saw* the sunlight shafting down through the leaves of the trees. She *wondered* at the lovely purple and white flowers whose names she didn't even know. She *smelled* the subtle scent of pine and honeysuckle. Brittany sat cross-legged on the concrete patio and stared and stared. She was entranced by the beauty and became awed by her participation in it. Brittany worshipped God.

This moment represented a shift in Brittany's way of perceiving the world. It was a joyous moment—a moment in which her longings and passions had been set free from unrealistic wishes and she could finally bring them to the real world.

What had happened? The brook, the tiny forest, the flowers, and the sun had all been there for years. She had purchased the house five years ago. Why was Brittany able to finally see the beauty and respond to her surroundings at this moment?

The shift in Brittany's way of seeing her world was not caused by an external event, accomplishment, goal, or person. Rather the shift happened because of significant changes *inside* Brittany. Slowly, imperceptibly, as she worked to gain insight into the distorted childhood happenings in her heart, Brittany began to appreciate her mother deeply just as she had in the early years of her childhood. This time, however, she looked at her mother with an adult's perspective. She saw the strength in her mother's love. She saw the wisdom in her kindness toward people. It dawned on Brittany that her mother had lived her life with real dignity and that her mother had succeeded in life. She saw that her mother's type of success was different from but in no way inferior to her father's success.

As she saw these things, a whole new view of the world began to open up to Brittany—a world she hadn't noticed in her driven pursuit to be a career woman. It was a world in which not only the tough and the strong attracted her but also the gentle and the tender. Those who could love with the relentless kind of love her mother had always had also began to appeal to her. In her attempt to distance herself from longings for her mother and to identify with an idealized father, Brittany had ignored those who knew how to love well. She had not given herself permission to experience the quiet joy of puttering around her home, sitting contentedly on her patio, and taking in the beauty of the simple things of life. As she began to connect once again with that priceless commodity called mother-love, a whole new world opened to her. The changes took place at the deepest levels of Brittany's soul.

Envy: A Special Type of Spoiling

The Latin word for envy comes from a verb meaning "to cast an evil eye upon."[1] Envy carries with it the idea of wanting to put a curse on another person or on something the other person has with the intent to destroy. Seeing another person have something special—whether it is a great relationship with parents or a spouse, a ritzy Mercedes, a prestigious career, or a wit that wins popularity with peers—prompts in the envious heart a longing that one believes cannot be filled. Seeing another revel in good fortune seems to highlight our own bad fortune. Watching someone else enjoy good things in life leaves us feeling we are all the more trapped in our own frustrated yearnings. So believing that we will feel more content with our lot in life if the other person doesn't seem so happy, we set out to lessen the gap between his or her good fortune and our limited fortune.

We may do this through making envious, spoiling statements (to ourselves or to others) such as, "He's so wealthy. I don't know where it came from. I wonder if he got it honestly." We might say, "Everybody thinks he's so funny. Personally, I think he's corny." Or we might comment, "I don't know why so many people come to hear him talk. He's good, but he's not *that* good." These are envious statements because they try to belittle another in order to allay our envy. When another has something we want, we make it seem less desirable through such spoiling statements, and thus, we are able to calm our discontent about that person's possessions or position.

Joseph of Old Testament fame had brothers who envied him and acted out their envy. They envied their father's favoritism of Joseph. They ridiculed Joseph as a conceited dreamer. So successfully did they in their own minds frame Joseph as a bad guy that they were able to sell him—their own brother—into slavery. Spoiling Joseph seemed easier than dealing with their disappointed longings for the special relationship they saw he had with their father.

Like all spoiling, envy blocks our joy. It's interesting to consider the alternative to envy. If we didn't envy other people's good news and didn't take it in as a threat to our own well-being, we could feel joy with them. Further, we might feel *inspired* by their good news and believe that it could happen to us as well.

It might look like this. A friend named Phil once did the unthinkable. As an amateur golfer with two years of playing golf under his belt, he went to a golf tournament at what was then El Toro Marine Base in California, and he made the prize-winning hole-in-one. He won a truck! Celebratory shouts echoed as news rippled around the golf course. Within five minutes everybody knew he had won the prize. People came up to him and said, "Are you the one?" Everyone at the golf course was exuberant that day. Someone had finally beat the odds. Nobody *ever* won the hole-in-one auto.

When Phil went to pick up his truck at the Ford dealership, salespeople flocked around and eagerly asked him, "Are you the one?" They pressed him for data. "What iron did you use? How did you swing it?" With their imaginary golf clubs, they reenacted the scene with him. As they made their imaginary strokes, they were sharing in Phil's joy and experiencing hope that perhaps such good fortune could one day come their way.

A lot of people experienced a lot of joy over my friend's hole-in-one. When God says, "Rejoice with those who rejoice" (Rom 12:15), he's not saying it because it's a good Christian exercise in selflessness to rejoice in another's promotion. He's saying it because it's a simple and obvious road to recurring joy. Somebody is always experiencing success, happiness, or good fortune. But we do not always let *good* be *good*. Rather we spoil it and make good out to be *bad* in order to ward off wishing or desiring.

Frustrated wishing and desiring can hurt or disappoint badly. So like the fox of Aesop's fables, we convince ourselves that the grapes hanging just out of reach were probably sour, and even if we could have attained them, we would not have liked them anyhow!

Wishing Away Our World

Splitting and spoiling are two ways of wishing that young children use to protect themselves. Unfortunately, these coping mechanisms really cost us when we reach adulthood. By splitting and spoiling, we pretend the real world—the world inside of ourselves as well as the outer world—does not exist. The real world, whether harshly negative or tantalizingly positive, just seems too threatening. So we *wish away* our threatening world. We blot it out through splitting or spoiling.

Even so, we panic as the reality we have so carefully cut out of our lives confronts us with emptiness and holes. Frantically and reflexively, we try to fill the holes through more defensive wishing. Then we reach the next line of defense in defensive wishing. We begin to wish for an ideal world filled with ideal people.

In the next chapter, we will see how our wishes for the ideal may seem like the only way to fill the voids left by the splitting and spoiling. We idealize, but once again…we do so at great cost to our souls.

CHAPTER 6

DEFENSIVE WISHING—
PART 3: WISHING FOR THE IDEAL

We see a poignant picture of this wishing for the ideal in an enchanting movie *Ladyhawke*. A knight and a lady were deeply in love. An evil bishop envied their love and sought to destroy it by a curse. The curse was ingeniously cruel. It kept the knight and lady ever in love with and longing for each other, but with fulfillment of that longing just beyond their reach.

Here's what happened. The lady, a lovely and beguiling woman by night, turned into a hawk by day, while the knight, an extremely handsome, well-built man by day, changed into a wolf by night. They were each other's constant companions but were unable to consummate their love.

This was not the most agonizing part of the curse, however. Each dawn and each dusk as they changed from human to animal and animal to human, the lady and the knight would see each other as human beings for one fleeting moment. They would reach out to each other, images shimmering out of time and space, longing for even just a moment of contact. (This is wishing for the ideal!) Then even as they almost touched, the possibility vanished. One became an animal, and the other became human.

As usually happens in fairy tales, there was eventually a happy ending. Wishes came true. Through amazing perseverance and remarkable circumstances (the gods were with this good couple!), the winsome couple was able to arrive at a certain castle at a certain time and (hallelujah chorus) undo the spell: Knight and lady, together at last, dancing, romancing, and in love forever.

A Child's Wish for the Ideal

Endings are not always so happy in the stories from our childhoods. Longings are just as intense, poignant, and unattainable as those of the lady and knight, but outcomes are not magical, not even when we pray to God.

In real family life, wishing for the ideal unfolds differently. The wish begins in a young child's heart, usually for a mother or a father whom the child thinks would be better than her real mother or father. The function of this defensive wish—as of all defensive wishes—is to ward off a painful reality through fantasy. The child constructs wishes for and fantasies of an ideal person in order to escape the pain of repeated losses inflicted by hurtful styles of interaction in her real family. The wish becomes the child's main defense against these hurts.

So far, so good. Again, this is necessary for survival. But children don't realize that these defensive wishes for ideal people are protective wishes. The imaginary friends stop being imaginary! Then these children grow up to be adults who still believe in and pursue these fanciful persons. They stay in love with wishes or wished-for people. Their passions and energies are solidly invested in this imaginary inner world, and they are trapped in attempting to recreate it. Their passions are not free to invest in real people and the real world around them. Their wishes become fortresses that protect them but also keep people out and leave them isolated.

Three Layers of Pain or Sadness

In addition to sidetracking our passions from real people, there are other problems when an adult wishes for the ideal. Our wishes, while *protecting* us from experiencing the full brunt of our hurts and sadness, also *prevent* us from working through these emotions. Ironically, our defensive wishes actually keep the hurts and sadness stored inside us in a kind of deep freeze.

One client came to see and understand this pattern in her own life. Jan was facing several intense losses and was afraid. She explained that her fear was not just of the losses themselves but of the *double pain* she kept digging herself into. "I create illusions to guard against the losses. Then I have a double pain to contend with—the disappointment of the illusions that don't come true *and* the original pain of the reality I was trying to escape."

Jan is so right. There is actually a triple sadness and pain maintained by defensive wishing. It involves

1. the disappointment of the defensive wishes that cannot come true;
2. the original sadness of the reality she was trying to escape, which she will not be able to face and work through until she gives up her defensive wishes; and,
3. the pain of the loneliness that results as she ignores the real people around her in her quest for the fantasy or the ideal person.

The pain maintained by Jan's wishing was this: Her mother had been harsh and unattainable, but only to Jan. Her mother idealized boys and adored Jan's older brother. She lavished all kinds of exciting and special attention on him. Jan watched with longing. She wished fervently for the kind of attention her brother was receiving. Over time her wishes became a quiet obsession. She was not even aware of her obsession. She had learned to keep her longings out of her conscious mind.

The longings were so tormenting that she would spoil and demean her mother. She would act as though she didn't want her. But deep in her soul, she had a fantasy that one day her harsh, unattainable mother would be transformed and suddenly bestow attention on her. This fantasy mother she created would publicly repent of her foolishness in having overlooked Jan's talents and gifts, and then she would demote her brother and promote Jan to compensate her for years of suffering.

This was Jan's wish for the ideal, and she continued to pursue it even after she had become an adult. In fact, this wish pervaded all her adult relationships. Like the lady and the knight reaching out longingly for each other at dawn and dusk, she continued to long intensely for the impossible. In pursuing her fantasy of an aloof mother who would see the error of her ways and suddenly change and make it all up to her daughter, Jan was always seeking relationships with aloof people—people who were not capable of closeness. Without realizing it or intending to, Jan locked herself into a world that was just like the deprived world of her childhood. While pursuing this unattainable wish for an aloof person, Jan was blotting out those people in her life who really *did* care about her. Jan had not been able to receive this love from her many friends because she pursued her wish for the ideal mother as if she were wearing blinders. It seemed to Jan that only an ideal mother could redeem her lost years of childhood and the shame and unfairness she had suffered. So Jan chose to overlook the love of her peers—love that could have healed her—to pursue relentlessly the love of an elusive mother. She hoped that this love, once found, would magically transform her.

Jan's defensive wishes were keeping her trapped in the three layers of pain. First, her original pain and sadness—that of playing second fiddle to a favored sibling—was being preserved because Jan postponed confronting and dealing with it. She simply wished it away. The pain of growing up with a favored sibling is like the adult experience of being deeply in love with someone and having that person fall in love with someone else. The difference is that as adults, if we work hard at it, we can face the sadness, let go, and switch romantic partners. Children cannot switch mommies. They are stuck wanting a special relationship with their mothers that they cannot have, and it feels unbearably sad. When children are that sad, they must construct defenses against their pain. This provides a psychological path out of their situation when they cannot physically leave it. Thus, defensive wishing rescues the child from the unbearable pain of the moment, but it can also prevent the child from working through his or her pain in the long run.

Second, Jan experienced ongoing disappointment as the unrealistic wishes she was pursuing did not come true. She repeatedly took her wishes for this ideal mother not only to her mother but to peers, teachers, and mentors as well. No matter how supportive these people wanted to be, none of them could transform themselves into an ideal parent who could redeem her childhood. Jan suffered repeated disappointments of her hopes.

Finally, Jan experienced the pain of the loneliness that came as she, in her single-minded pursuit of an ideal mother, shunned all the real humans who could and did love her.

Understanding the Cost

The resolution of the sadness and pain kept alive by wishing for an unattainable ideal will be examined in section 3. For now, it is enough to begin to understand the cost of being caught up in wishing for ideal people. Understanding the cost can prompt us to give up (to mourn) our unrealistic wishes. Mourning then frees us to turn our passions into reality. We are able to wish realistically and to see our wishes fulfilled.

In Stephen King's novel *Needful Things*,[1] a whole town is obsessed with wish fulfillment. People feverishly pursue their wishes—desires that have crept into their souls and taken possession. They *must* have the objects of their desires—those *needful things*—at any cost. The costs they inflict on one another and on themselves are brutal.

King provides us with a brilliant but awful caricature of what happens when we pursue unrealistic wishes without sensing their unreality and letting go of them. Usually, the outcome is not as evil or as deadly as the outcomes portrayed in this book. Usually, when we pursue unrealistic wishes and remain unwilling to let go of them, we simply become mired in frustration. For most, the dead end of this pursuit is depression, bitterness, and shame. We will explore the genesis of these emotions in the following chapters.

CHAPTER 7

DEPRESSION: THE CHRONIC MOURNING OF UNREALISTIC WISHES

Amid the sparkle of champagne and the rowdy toots of party favors, Connie was lost in a reverie. It was her thirtieth birthday party. People who loved her were celebrating enthusiastically, but Connie was distracted. She was looking intently inward, gone from the moment. As she looked within, she saw herself—a struggling little girl, the middle of three daughters, who always longed for her mother's love and attention. Connie always saw herself as being on the periphery of an impenetrable wall around her mother—a wall formed by her favored sisters.

Connie saw that struggling, longing little girl enter womanhood and meet an adoring man who treated her as though she were very special. Never mind that he was married and would never quite leave his wife—she saw the eighteen-year-old woman transfer her longings for specialness with her mother directly to this man. Then she relived the tantalizing unfulfilled promises he had made. She felt the torment of her longing, first for her mother and then for this man—longing that went on and on. And the man? He was still around, always *promising* to become available to her but never really *doing* it.

Connie's story is another example of defensive wishing. As an adult, Connie was expressing her unfulfilled longings from childhood. She directed her wishes toward a married man so that she wouldn't have to face the reality that her childhood wishes had not come true. She didn't want to face the fact that her mother had never become available to her in the ways she wanted. But Connie's defensive wishing didn't resolve her unfulfilled childhood wishes; it merely postponed her need to deal with those wishes.

Further, the defensive wishing created problems of its own. For Connie, the defensive wishing was creating an ongoing sadness over an unresolved loss. She had been sad for twelve years as she pursued a wish that wasn't going to come true. This man was never going to marry her. (And even if he did, she would find that her longings continued to be strangely unfulfilled.) A twelve-year-long sadness is not the normal sadness of a healthy mourning process. It is not loving, losing, letting go, and freeing up our energies to love again. A sadness that has continued for twelve years has settled into the chronic mourning of depression.

Healthy Mourning v. Chronic Mourning

The normal sadness of loving, losing, and letting go—healthy mourning—is a perfectly natural response to loss. When healthy people mourn, they are very painfully sad, less interested in the outside world, less loving, and less active.[1]

The last three characteristics of mourning stem from the fact that our energy must be turned inward in order to resolve our loss. We are focused on mourning and letting go of whatever or whomever we have lost. For a time, our energy is simply not available to invest in the outer world.

There is an unresolved or chronic mourning that has the same four characteristics but which differs from healthy mourning. Chronic mourning, which many psychologists believe to be an explanation for depression, is what we experience when we continue pursuing unrealistic wishes. Chronic mourning differs from healthy mourning in the following ways:

Healthy Mourning	Chronic Mourning
1. Is time limited	1. Goes on and on
2. Lets go of the lost love	2. Holds on to the lost love in the form of a wish
3. Frees up passion for reinvestment in new (real) loves.	3. Keeps passion tied up in the wish

As Connie continues to wish that this elusive married man will leave his wife and live happily ever after with her, she is locked into chronic mourning. She has been pursuing this wish and mourning its disappointment for twelve years.

Her defensive wishes have now become addictive and difficult to relinquish. Her fantasies toward this man may have become a reward in themselves. When she envisions their future together, she feels more alive than she ever has before. The soothing fantasies of an idyllic life together seem to blot out the stark, anguished reality of the lonely times between her brief encounters with him. There is more. The intense, exciting fantasies of life with this man also blot out the emptiness of her childhood (even while maintaining the emptiness). Connie has become hooked on her own wishes and fantasies. The wishes feel good, and they have taken on a life of their own.

She faces a dilemma—a dilemma *always* created by defensive wishes. Her wishes are unrealistic, and she is doomed to a lifetime of sadness if she does not give them up. But in order to resolve this ongoing sadness, Connie will have to face even deeper sadness—the profound sorrow of letting go of her wishes and of the man behind the wishes. She will also have to face the unresolved sadness from childhood that her relationship with this man has been covering up.

Connie's thirtieth birthday helped her face her dilemma and transform her chronic mourning into healthy mourning. She could finally let go of her wishes for this man. Her birthday nudged her toward reality. Since she was five years of age, she had always envisioned herself married and with children by the time she was thirty. But here she was, celebrating her thirtieth birthday and nowhere near marriage. The birthday was a stern, unrelenting reminder that life was passing her by. However loudly her wish promised to come true tomorrow—tomorrow, tomorrow—her birthday party cued her that her tomorrows were slipping away. Wishes may never pass away, but childbearing years do. She wanted to have some *realized* dreams to look back on by the time she was forty. Facing this fact, Connie began to say the most agonizing goodbye of her life.

Biblical Examples of Healthy and Chronic Mourning

Connie's struggle with the broken promises of an affair provide an excellent example of how chronic mourning can be transformed into healthy mourning. Other examples of chronic and healthy mourning are found in scripture, namely in the lives of the patriarch Jacob and of King David.

Jacob is the example of chronic mourning. Responding to news that his favorite son, Joseph, was dead, "Jacob tore his clothes, and put sackcloth on his loins, and mourned for his son many days" (Gn 37:34). In tearing his clothes, Jacob is following traditional Jewish custom and symbolizing his loss in concrete ways that will help him face the reality that something awful has happened. "Then all his sons and all his daughters arose to comfort him ..." (v.35).

Comforters are pivotal in coming to grips with loss, and here the mourning process is still going as well as can be expected. Then a problem arises: "...but he refused to be comforted. And he said, 'Surely I will go down to Sheol in mourning for my son.' So his father [Jacob] wept for him [Joseph]" (v. 35).

This may be simply the anguished statement of a man in the initial throes of profound grief. But in his refusal to be comforted and in his commitment to a lifetime of mourning, Jacob seems to be engaging in chronic rather than healthy mourning. In healthy mourning, the mourner comes to grips with the loss of someone who has died. His grief gradually lessens as he slowly lets go of wishes for a future with that person. But so far Jacob refuses to let go of his wishes for a future with his son. Grief is actually a way of maintaining our bond with the one who has died, and Jacob vows he will mourn for Joseph until he dies. He will continue his relationship with his son. The problem is that there can be no real relationship. As long as he mourns, Jacob's passions will be tied up in an intensely wished-for relationship with a son who has died.

Perhaps Jacob is angrily protesting the loss as something that never should have happened, and since it should not have happened, he simply refuses to come to grips with it. Ongoing protest is often a part of the chronic mourner's stance.

Or perhaps Jacob is too overwhelmed to face yet another loss. He already lost his beloved wife Rachel in childbirth to Joseph's younger brother. To now lose one of their only two children could seem unbearable--impossible to face.

Present grief is compounded by past grief. The effect can be immeasurable, beyond words, and very difficult to overcome. The point is not to judge Jacob; there is not a right or wrong way to grieve. Our ways of grieving are deeply personal and should never be judged. Jacob responded to overwhelming circumstances the best he knew how. But insofar as he persists over time in his refusal to be comforted and in his commitment to perpetual mourning for

Joseph, his grief will settle into the relentless ache and heaviness of a deep, unremitting depression.

King David, on the other hand, seems to illustrate healthy mourning rather than chronic mourning. In 2 Samuel 12:15–24, David's manner of dealing with the impending death of his infant son—after he was informed by a prophet the baby would die—is important. He feels very intensely about his impending loss, and he disengages from his world. He does not eat or talk with his servants. He ceases all activity and lies prostrate on the ground. His focus is toward God on behalf of the cherished baby. David's actions seem to depict all four characteristics of the mourning described previously. He is very painfully sad, less interested in the outside world, less loving, and less active.

Then the child dies, and the servants are afraid to tell David. His reaction has been so intense thus far that they fear he might harm himself if he knows that his son has actually died.

From their whisperings, David surmises that the baby has died. So he gets up from the ground, washes himself, and changes his clothes. He worships God and then goes home to eat.

The servants are confused, and they ask David why he has decided to get up and eat now that the child has died. Why was he so distraught when the child was still alive?

David replies to their questions, "While the child was still alive, I fasted and wept; for I said, 'Who knows, the Lord may be gracious to me, that the child may live.' But now he has died; why should I fast? Can I bring him back again? I shall go to him, but he will not return to me" (2 Sm 12:22, 23).

David had the same wishes for a future with his son that Jacob had. But David's mourning process was different. David accepted the reality that the future with his son, for which he had so fervently wished, was not to be. In accepting the reality of his loss, David let go of his son. Or better stated, he let go of his wish for a life with his son. It is in this mourning and letting go that the longings and wishes David had for his baby boy are freed up to be invested in other people. "Then David comforted his wife Bathsheba, and went in to her and lay with her; and she gave birth to a son, and he named him Solomon" (v. 24).

David went full cycle through the mourning process. He focused intensely on his loss, he let go, and he reinvested his longings in available loves. Although the mourning process usually does not occur this quickly, David's resolution of his loss seems to be genuine. Resolution of a loss does not mean the mourner will feel no more sadness over the loss. It means that he or she has worked through the most intense part of the sadness. The worst is over. And now the mourner has freed up his or her passion to be invested in other loves. It also means that the mourner will not be plagued by the dull, unrelenting sadness of depression that so many suffer because they cannot bear to face and work through the full magnitude of their losses.

It is important to restate that the mourning process usually does not occur as quickly as it did for David. Many of us, facing the traumatic loss of a child, would stumble in and out of crushing grief for a very long time. A parent suffering the loss of a child (or a child losing a parent) is among the most dreaded losses. Facing such a loss, we are forever changed and might in some sense never get over it. Nonetheless, if we keep facing the reality of our loss, with lots of help from wise friends who comfort well, we, like David, can get to a point where we let go of our crippling sadness and pressing wishes for ongoing relationship with the deceased and are freed up to move forward with our current loved ones and renewed purpose in life. That purpose may revolve around the deceased—consider Mothers Against Drunk Drivers or AMBER Alert. But we can regain the energy to move forward into a meaningful life.

A Further Look at the Healthy Mourning
of Unrealistic Wishes Left by Loss

In loss, our outer reality has changed. The change may have been abrupt or gradual, but the final loss is drastic. People we loved dearly and deeply are gone. But though our outward reality clearly has changed, our inner reality remains the same. Our inner bond with the departed people lives vibrantly on. Vividly, we remember the life we shared, and each memory holds wishes, longings, and expectations for life as always with our dear ones. It may happen like this: Awakening after a joyous reunion, we slowly realize it was just a dream. Visiting an old haunt, we're sure we see them until reality sinks in. A phone rings, and for a nanosecond we expect it to be a call from the people we've lost. Painfully, we reorient to a life without them...again and again. We wrapped our lives and dreams around a future with the person who has died (or left in some other way), and we relinquish our wishes and dreams for that future reluctantly and with much sorrow.

Healthy mourning is the process of letting ourselves feel—cry, weep, rage, protest, pound pillows, and repeatedly face the outer reality that they're gone—as our inner reality slowly catches up with the outer reality. In his stirringly hopeful autobiography titled *A Severe Mercy*, Sheldon Vanauken illustrates this process poignantly and realistically. His book is the story of the sweet, unshakeable love that Vanauken and his wife Davy forged and his coming to grips with her loss when she died far too young. He committed to grieving for his wife as wholeheartedly as he had loved her, and he shares hard-fought lessons about dealing with memories and the wishes and longings they hold.

Devastated by Davy's death, Vanauken immersed himself in grief before returning to classes at the university where he taught. Unexpectedly, he found that returning to the structure of his classes helped. For a moment he was lost in his old routine. Smiling with students, calmly reading poetry (even about loss!), he experienced a reprieve from the intense grief. But at the end of the day, preparing to return home, he was flooded with grief as he faced his little MG car. The MG held such pleasant memories of drives with his wife in the countryside, their dog Flurry alongside, ears blowing in the wind. They had even very intentionally taken a final drive in the car to have their own farewell rite before she died. And now he was facing the MG *without his wife*. The grief was overwhelming.

The next day, going out to the car after teaching, he was prepared for crushing grief. But grief didn't come in the same way. What he realized was that he had to face the MG without his wife one time and take it through what he called "a piercingly bleak emptiness,"[2] and then it no longer held the same power to overwhelm him with sadness. But he also realized that "thousands of other things and memories"[3] from his shared life with Davy would flood over him just like the MG had and that each one of them would need to go through the "piercingly bleak emptiness"[2] in the excruciating process of coming to grips with the loss of his wife.

There are indeed "thousands of other things and memories"[3] we must face and mourn in the heartbreaking process of grief— memories woven around countless shared experiences with our lost loved ones: the once happy smell of a favorite holiday dish; that worn, carefully molded La-Z-Boy chair, now empty; summertime with its reminder of adventures, banding together against the rugged outdoors; his first birthday without her, her first birthday without him; insider jokes that bring a smile before the flood of tears; or the refrain of that special song playing unexpectedly. Such memories hold traditions—things richly enjoyed over and over again—which carry the deeply imbedded wish and anticipation that this cherished memory will surely happen again. Faithfully, these memories need to be taken through the "piercingly bleak emptiness."[2] We must experience the acute, searing reality that our loved ones are gone, and these memories will not actually happen ever again.

It seems like an unbearable process, but there are two very hopeful outcomes in grieving like Vanauken grieved. First, we come to accept the reality that our loved ones are gone. Our inner reality comes to match our outer reality, and however fundamentally we may have changed through the shattering loss, our wishes and passions are now freed up to bring to reality. Released from the chronic mourning of depression, we are ready to move forward, living and loving fully in the actual life that remains for us.

The second outcome is that having taken the memories through the "piercingly bleak emptiness,"[2] we are free to simply enjoy our memories of a lost loved one. No longer so loaded with sadness, the memories don't have the same power to sabotage and overwhelm us. We don't need to keep them out of mind in order to prevent a downward spiral into grief. We can simply delight in remembering the unique closeness, shared laughter and tears, or quirky, fun things we enjoyed together. In this way, our memories come to nourish and enrich our lives and strengthen us going forward, which is exactly what rich memories are supposed to do.

CHAPTER 8

BITTERNESS: A RESERVOIR OF ANGER OVER WISHES THAT HAVEN'T COME TRUE

The biblical story of Naomi is a good illustration of the workings of bitterness. A famine struck Naomi's homeland, Judah. So with her husband and two sons, she left Bethlehem in Judah to go to Moab. I can imagine Naomi settling with her family in Moab but still missing her native country. Perhaps she was intrigued with the customs of this new land. Perhaps she tried hard to learn them so that she could engage wholeheartedly in her new life. In time she adjusted to the changes, but she may well have had certain unstated wishes that many of us today share about our own futures. She may have wished for predictability and sameness. She may have wished that good times with loved ones would continue uninterrupted. In the face of the disruption and losses she had recently experienced in her forced move to Moab, Naomi's wishes may have been especially intense. Like many of us, she probably also dreamed of living a long, rich life surrounded by maturing children and adoring grandchildren and eventually being buried by these children. But Naomi's wishes were not to come true.

Naomi lost both her husband and then her sons to death. Scripture sums up Naomi's devastating losses in a line so simple and straightforward that we might miss the depth and pathos behind it. "The woman was bereft of her two children and her husband" (Ru 1:5). Naomi now had no hope for the future that she had planned for, counted on, and desired with all her heart. Everything had changed. She decided it was best to go home.

It is in this context that we encounter a famous line in scripture. Naomi's daughters-in-law wanted to accompany her on her return to Judah. For their sakes, she bids them to stay behind in their homeland of Moab. In response to Naomi's urgings, Ruth makes the statement that has been repeated in many wedding ceremonies as an avowal of unswerving loyalty: "Do not urge me to leave you or turn back from following you; for where you go, I will go, and where you lodge, I will lodge. Your people shall be my people, and your God, my God" (Ru 1:16). Ruth and Naomi continue on to Judah, while Orpah, Naomi's other daughter-in-law, turns back.

In spite of Ruth's touching commitment to Naomi, when Naomi arrives in her homeland and people greet her by name, she makes a telling statement: "Do not call me Naomi [pleasant]; call me Mara [bitter], for the Almighty has dealt very bitterly with me" (Ru 1:20). Naomi had the fierce loyalty of her daughter-in-law, but that did not begin to compensate for the loss of a husband and two sons. Naomi's greatest wishes in life were denied her. Further, she interpreted her losses as God being against her. She was bitter.

Naomi illustrates the bitterness that can come when our deepest wishes and dreams have been denied us. Bitterness has been a part of human experience from the time of Cain and Abel.

The Experience of Bitterness

What exactly is bitterness, and how do we become embittered? Like depression, bitterness also begins with frustrated wishes. When we continue to pursue wishes that are not coming true, we experience not only the ongoing sadness and disappointment of depression; we also experience an ongoing frustration and anger that settle into bitterness.

Bitterness then is a reservoir of anger over disappointed wishes. Often the anger has been accumulating for a lifetime. The bitter person has been angry so long that he or she is perhaps no longer even aware of the anger.

I once was talking with a man whose frowning countenance gave away his anger as he dully recounted things that had gone wrong in his life. I reflected casually, "You seem angry." He denied being angry. So I told him some of the cues I was seeing that told me he was angry. He slammed his fist down on the table and shouted at me, *"I'm not angry!"* He was not lying. He had been angry so long that his anger had come to feel like life as usual.

Bitter people not only have trouble recognizing their own anger, but they also have trouble expressing it. They overreact to little irritations. They fume over little things like congested traffic, having to wait in line, a waitress making a mistake, or a copier being out of paper. These little mishaps are tapping into a huge reservoir of anger.

Furthermore, these people get caught in a double bind. Struggling under a heavy weight of unresolved anger, they are so prone to rage that it feels as if they have only two options in expressing even mild aggravation—be silent or kill. They will either get so angry they explode in an inappropriate fit, or fearing this extreme, they withdraw in icy silence. For example, it would be nice to be able to remind the waitress that they ordered a rare steak, but even a simple, everyday assertion like that would come out in such hostile, overbearing tones that they don't dare open their mouths. Thus, bitter people often stew in silent but intense anger. As the anger accumulates, eventually they *do* explode.

Bitterness creates a downward spiral of less and less wish fulfillment. Bitter people angrily demand that other people (and events) change to fulfill their wishes. They get caught in a cycle of blaming other people for their own disappointments. They end up alienating people and getting less and less of what they want from others.

A Decision Tree of Wishing: To Mourn or Not to Mourn

As illustrated in the following decision tree, we have choices regarding our wishes. We can bitterly demand their fulfillment. Or when they involve other people, we can express them as requests, and then we can mourn and let go of them if they are denied us.

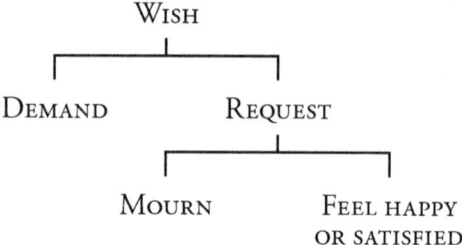

Consider a simple, everyday example of a wish. Jean had a difficult day at work, was feeling quite vulnerable, and deeply longed to be held by her husband John. That was her wish.

Starting at the right side of the previously outlined decision tree, a healthy way to express her wish would be to make the following request: "Honey, I'd love to curl up on your lap. Could I?" In putting her wish into request form in this way, Jean would be doing two things.

First, she would communicate clearly her wish to John. Expressing our wishes clearly is pivotal to getting what we want. It is an important form of self-assertion. But we may balk at doing this. Perhaps we want our wishes to be known without having to ask (another unrealistic wish!). Or perhaps we are afraid of feeling vulnerable and exposed. It may seem as if we are giving the other person the power to hurt or even shame us when we express our deepest longings.

Second, in expressing her wish as a request, Jean would be acknowledging that her husband is a separate person with wishes of his own. He has a right to choose; he has the right to turn down her request.

At this point, one of two things could happen in response to Jean's request. Her husband could say yes, and Jean would then curl up on his lap and feel happy (or soothed). Her wish would have come true.

Or her husband could say no, and Jean would then feel quite sad (and would mourn) that he did not want to give her what she wanted. If she could accept his saying no—and mourn and let go of her wishes—she would not become bitter. Bitterness comes from hanging on to wishes and insisting they come true even after they have been denied us.

It is as simple as that on the surface. But Jean, who was quite good at self-assertion and had even taught courses in it, could not express her own wish as a request. She could not allow the possibility of a negative answer. We, too, often go to great lengths to avoid hearing no. It's risky to allow the other person the chance to say no to our deep longings. We open ourselves up to the possibility of intense sadness.

Further, our wishes—what we deeply desire in life—are about as close to our heart as we get. Because our wishes are so deeply personal, we often take it very personally when they are rejected. It's as though the rejection said something about us, about our being undeserving or unworthy. This is especially true when we have suffered too many uncomforted losses in childhood, as Jean had. It can feel as though we have surpassed our quota of losses, and we simply cannot tolerate another rejection or loss.

So we try to avoid this risk. We may avoid it by convincing ourselves and others that we do not wish for anything at all— nothing ventured, nothing gained, nothing lost. (Actually, avoidance is a third alternative on the previously outlined decision tree—to just blot out our wish from the beginning and stop the whole process. But this is only a mask to our underlying wishes and bitterness.)

Entitlement and Bitterness

Conversely, starting at the left side of the decision tree, we may turn our wishes into demands. We may try to take away the other person's right to say no. When we do this, we are expressing a sense of entitlement.

Entitlement goes hand in hand with bitterness. When we feel entitled, we have deeply ingrained wishes or illusions that we deserve better than we have had so far. We believe that life owes us a payback. In *The Screwtape Letters*, C. S. Lewis aptly captures the connection between entitlement and bitterness. A senior devil instructs a junior devil, "Men are not angered by mere misfortune but by misfortune conceived as injury. And the sense of injury depends on feeling that a legitimate claim has been denied. The more claims on life, therefore, that your patient can be induced to make, the more often he will feel injured and, as a result, ill-tempered."[1]

These "claims on life" prompt us to insist on the fulfillment of our wishes—to go on pursuing unrealistic wishes—rather than mourning and letting go of them at appropriate times. They are indeed pivotal to bitterness.

Jean was about to make such claims on life. She was about to coerce John into giving her the hug, to which she felt *entitled*. As with all defensive wishing, Jean's entitlement wishes protected her in a way. As a child, Jean lacked physical affection from her mother. Thus, in her sense of entitlement, she fully believed she was guaranteed hugs as a payback for her childhood losses and that these hugs in adulthood could somehow make up for the past neglect in her life.

All her life Jean has been waiting for payoffs. She has been living in constant expectation that she will finally get all the good things she deserves to make up for all the bad things she did not deserve. This expectation or wish for a future that will compensate for her past has protected her from dealing with the simple reality that she has suffered grave loss. Unfortunately, our sense of being owed turns our wishes into demands, and we end up angry and bitter when we don't get what we want.

Wish Turned into Demand

Believing that she is owed what she deeply desires, Jean *demands* that her wishes be granted. She expresses her wishes in a way that coerces, manipulates, or emotionally blackmails her husband into giving her what she wants. There are many different ways she could word her demand to John. She could phrase her wish in a way that frames him as bad if he doesn't want to hug her. She could tell him she hopes he's not going to be his usual cold-fish self and refuse to hug her. She could keep nagging him until he holds her just to shut her up. She could threaten (between the lines) that she has trouble performing sexually when she's not had enough affection. Or she could simply imply that he is violating his marital vows if he does not hold her.

What Jean actually *did* was a subtler, nicer way of manipulating John, but it was still manipulation. Jean and her husband were at a marital seminar. Couples were discussing the unfulfilled longings within their marriages. The wives were complaining that their husbands didn't talk or cuddle enough, and several of the women had resorted to overeating to soothe their unmet longings. Jean was one of these women. When John and Jean were married, Jean had been very slender, but she had consistently put on weight. She had noticed that one of the situations in which she would get *uncontrollable* cravings for food was when John was emotionally distant from her.

At the seminar we traced those cravings back to childhood. Jean came to understand that her overeating had its origins in her early relationship with her mother. Her mother had been an efficient, proper woman who faithfully met her children's needs but was stiff and infrequent with her hugs. Jean had always dreamed of the day when she would meet someone like her warmly affectionate father. Then, she reasoned, she would finally get all the physical affection she wanted. These wistful fantasies had soothed the longings that her mother had thwarted. In fact, as a teenager, Jean had been obsessed with having a perfect body so she could find a perfect man who could finally make up for all the affection she lacked from her mother. (She ate too little and became quite thin.)

She thought John was that perfect man, and she married him. But now John seemed frighteningly similar to her mother. Jean despaired and turned to food—which she *could* control—to soothe her longings. The result was the weight gain.

In a group session with her husband and other couples, Jean put together her insights astutely in a very subtle but manipulative demand that John grant her wishes. "Honey, we've discovered that my overeating relates to Mom's not hugging me as a child. So what I need from you when I'm craving food is to be held." She was translating her *wish* into a *need* in an effort to make her wish more compelling. In this way, she could leave her husband feeling obligated to hold her. She was stating her unresolved longings from childhood in a way that made them her husband's problem and his responsibility to solve. A couple of women nodded their heads emphatically in agreement with Jean's dilemma.

I then glanced at John. He squirmed with an uncomfortable look on his face. The look said, "What decent husband would refrain from helping his wife cure an eating disorder? But I don't want to hug her." So we explored John's feelings about hugging. When he was a young boy, his mother had given him marvelous, warm hugs.

But then when he was only three years of age, his older brother—who was like a father to him in many ways—began shaming him, calling him a "momma's boy" and a "sissy" for being so affectionate with his mother. Little John still wanted the hugs, but he began to recoil from them because the shame he felt from his brother's remarks overpowered his longings to be hugged.

A Double Bind

So we had a problem. Based on her unmet needs from childhood, Jean *needed* to be hugged. Based on his unmet needs from childhood, John *needed* not to hug. This seemed like a stalemate.

But the double bind created by Jean's demands goes even deeper. In demanding rather than requesting that her husband hug her, Jean blocks the one thing she really wants—to feel chosen, loved, and wanted by her husband. For if her husband hugs her in response to a demand, the meaning of the hug changes. Jean then believes he has no choice, that she has forced him to hug her. This may be great for her sense of control, but it hurts her sense of being loved and wanted.

Whatever the specific contents of our wishes, this is the bottom-line wish we all have: We want to feel wanted. We want to feel chosen, loved, or cherished by someone we also cherish. But if we cannot tolerate no, we can never get a wholehearted yes. If we are not willing to let the other person have a choice (which means we must be willing to risk having our wishes turned down and then having to mourn our lost wishes), we can never know what it feels like to be chosen, loved, and wanted—even if we get the hugs.

Resolution

The way out of these double binds is for both Jean and John to face and mourn their unresolved wishes from childhood so that they are free to be with each other in their honest adult longings as man and woman. For her part, Jean needs to learn to grieve in response to her husband's rejection of her wishes. In learning to tolerate and to grieve the rejection of her everyday wishes, she also needs to confront the grief behind the grief—the deep sadness over her mother's lack of physical affection and emotional presence when Jean was very young.

As Jean faces, mourns, and works through these childhood longings, the wishes she has toward John will lose their intensity—that sense of "I *have* to have this." She will no longer need to pressure him, framing him as a bad guy in order to get what she's wanting. (Unwittingly, Jean has been shaming John—just as his older brother did—as she tries to coerce a hug.) She will be able to honestly put her wishes as requests, allowing John the freedom to choose.

Then John might experience increased freedom to say no. He might find the freedom to explore his own motives and hang-ups behind his resistance to hugging. He might be able to face and mourn his own unresolved longings for admiration from his older brother. He might be able to give up pretending he didn't need or want his mother when he really did. Unconscious efforts to win his brother's admiration had continued throughout John's life and were now being expressed in emotional distance from his wife. If John were willing and able to look honestly into his own soul apart from external pressure, he might be able to say, "Jean, I love you. I wish I could hug you. But I just can't right now because there is so much shame wrapped up in hugging a woman. The image of my ridiculing brother is still strong."

If Jean could allow John the space to choose, she might not get her hugs immediately. But John and Jean could get something deeper, more real, and more gratifying. They could begin being more genuinely present to each other. They could become two people honestly struggling to get to know each other, to understand each other, and to try to work out ways of honoring each other's deepest longings. This is what intimacy is all about. This is wanting and being wanted. This is wish fulfillment, and it has very little to do with hugs.

Again, the cruel irony of our entitlement—of demanding that our wishes be granted us—is that we unwittingly kill any chance to have what we are truly wanting in our very efforts to ensure we get it. The point of learning to mourn and let go of our unrealistic wishes is not just so that we might become stronger and more stoic. The point is that as we let go of unrealistic wishes, we become free to create and pursue wishes that *can* come true. Just as surely as "Hope deferred makes the heart sick," so too, "Desire fulfilled is a tree of life" (Prv 13:12).

CHAPTER 9

SHAME AND OUR DISAPPOINTED WISHES TO BE IDEAL

I once met a man who was born without arms. He had learned to adapt to life in very ingenious ways. For example, when drinking a cup of coffee at a social affair, he slipped off his shoe, brought his foot to the cup, grasped the handle with his toes, and brought the cup to his lips. Throughout this process he chatted amicably with the people around him. I admired him—not just his physical prowess but his emotional prowess as well. How had he learned to be so free and natural with such a marked handicap? How had he overcome the potential shame of it?

He had been handicapped from birth. I wondered if he had to work through the shame of ridicule by insensitive children who simply didn't understand such a handicap. Had he ever struggled with the shame of being treated as inferior by people who saw him as an easy target for their own despised weaknesses? Did he have to deal with the shame of being sometimes pitied and sometimes pampered by people who needed to feel needed but who subtly demeaned him in the process? I do not know what this man actually went through in overcoming his handicap. I'm just speculating on what he might have endured. Clearly there should be no shame in being handicapped. But I would guess he had to work through repeated bouts of severe shame that could easily have caused him to withdraw from people and from life. It was shame—and not just the physical handicap, as great as it was—that may have had the most potential to cripple him.

We are all like this man. We share in his humanity and we share in his brokenness. For many of us, the brokenness is not as visible and concrete as this man's. Nonetheless, our souls are far more handicapped than his body was. In fact, Henri Nouwen uses the brokenness of handicapped people as an image of the common brokenness we all share.[1] We are all very broken both because of our own sinfulness and because of wounds left by the sinfulness of others. Dr. Henry Cloud aptly describes this brokenness in his book *Changes that Heal.*[2] We are broken people, and it is this brokenness that often leads to the shame experience.

The Shame Experience

Shame is not a logical conclusion to our brokenness. Instead it is a highly illogical conclusion, but it is a conclusion most of us reach about our brokenness. Our beliefs about our brokenness and the feelings that accompany those beliefs make up the shame experience.

The bottom-line belief of shame is that I am broken *and* I am alone in my brokenness. If I could simply believe that all of us are struggling together in brokenness (which is the truth), I would not experience shame. In the shame experience, I view other people as being whole and vibrant, while I am alone in my brokenness. It is as though I struggle with a defectiveness unique to me.

As a corollary to this belief, I mistakenly believe that belonging and love are based on my being unbroken—perfect, together, whole. In his book *Orthodoxy and the Romance of Faith*, C. S. Lewis's mentor, G. K. Chesterton, writes that the secret of the story of *Beauty and the Beast* is that we have to be loved in order to be loveable.[3] This is a profound truth, and it is clearly also the truth of the gospel.

In the shame experience we twist this truth and say that we have to be loveable in order to be loved. But we cannot make ourselves loveable. A leopard cannot change his spots (see Jer 13:23), and neither can we. We cannot heal our own wounds and our own sinfulness. So the beliefs behind shame seem to pose an irresolvable dilemma. I feel myself to be uniquely bad, an outcast who is unworthy and outside the club of humanity with no way of gaining membership.

To further complicate things, because of these beliefs—that I am alone in my brokenness and I must be unbroken in order to be acceptable—I go into hiding with my defect. My secret defect must not be revealed at any cost. Thus, when I meet new people or try to form friendships, I concentrate on hiding my defect rather than on making myself known to the other person. Because I am so determined to hide, I end up feeling alienated and isolated. I then interpret this isolation as active rejection by other people. The isolation, which I myself unwittingly have created, becomes a confirmation of my own beliefs that I am uniquely defective and unworthy.

At this point I am in the downward spiral of shame. I have set things up so that I will slide deeper and deeper into shame and isolation. How do I get out? Somehow the man who had been born without arms had resisted this cycle of ever-increasing shame. He had not withdrawn from life and from people. He was an ordained priest, had been invited to meet with the president and the pope, and had authored several books. Somehow he had managed to stay in the mainstream of life and had developed both character and compassion. He had not dedicated his life to running from his brokenness. He had not let it define him. He had learned to embrace his brokenness and to get beyond it.

The secret to resolving our shame is learning to embrace our brokenness. In order to be able to embrace our brokenness and work through our shame, we first need to understand the mechanisms of shame—how it is created and maintained by unrealistic wishes just like depression and bitterness.

Moments of Shame

A pastor's simple sermon is preached straight from his heart to the congregation. The sermon is stunning in its simplicity, straightforwardness, and truth. The congregation sits, impacted deeply, trying to let the truth sink in, trying not to lose the richness of the pastor's words. They are so absorbed in mulling over new insights that they remain in their pews straight through the altar call, looking inward, lost in dialogue with God.

The next day is "blue Monday" for the pastor—the Monday after the Sunday when nobody came forward at the altar call. He sits alone in his study, head buried in his hands, lamenting his lack of skill as a pastor, chastising his inability to stir people, woefully wondering when he'll ever get it right. He is feeling inadequate and defective. The pastor is experiencing a moment of shame.

On another occasion, a very talented woman gives a piano concert. Her performance is excellent with only a few minor mistakes that go unnoticed by the wildly enthusiastic audience. "What passion!" "What poise!" "Best interpretation of Rachmaninoff ever." So go their spontaneous exclamations.

But the woman is backstage—pacing, wrenching her hands, chagrined. "How could I make those mistakes? When will I play it right? I can't believe I blew it again! This has got to stop! I never should have presumed to be a pianist. I can't believe it."

In reality, the pastor and the pianist did fine jobs. The people listening to them were blessed and enriched by their contributions. But each suffered shame—a sense of badness and inadequacy. Where does the sense of badness and inadequacy come from? Compared to whom and according to what standards were their performances *no good*?

Shame and the Ideal Self

It is only in light of their wishes to be ideal that these performances fall short. The burden that both the pastor and the pianist are laboring under is not the burden of public opinion or of objective reality. It is the burden of an inner insistence on perfection, which renders a very good performance shamefully inadequate. That's what *perfectionism* is—a wish to be so perfect that we beat ourselves up every time we make a tiny mistake. The pastor and the pianist are not even aware of their hidden wishes to be ideal. All they are aware of is a feeling of failure. Unknowingly, they are both pursuing a wish for an ideal self. It is this wish to be ideal that prompts painful self-criticism even in the face of very good performances.

The Three Selves of Shame[4]

Although our wishes for an ideal self are key in our feelings of shame, it is actually an interplay of three different ways of viewing ourselves that produces shame, namely

- the ideal (all-good) self,
- the real self, and
- the all-bad self.

First, these three selves will be defined. Then we will look at how they interact to create the shame experience.

We all start with a real self. The real self is who I really am—an intricate blend of strengths and weaknesses. I am created in the image of God, but I am also utterly sinful. My intense pursuit of God is often dampened by my own hateful, hurtful behavior. I do marvelous, precocious things, and I make stupid mistakes. In one way or another, this is the real self we all have to work with.

We also develop an ideal self as we grow. This is the self we wish we were. Naturally, there is a gap between the real and the ideal—between who we are and who we wish we were. Striving to fulfill our wishes for an ideal self can be healthy. Reaching beyond ourselves to embrace ideals allows a transcending of ourselves that promotes growth, wholeness, and goodness in our lives. The problem in our pursuit of wishes to be more ideal comes when we try to blot out reality in pursuit of our wishes. Then our wishes become defensive (designed to protect us from reality) rather than realistic (designed to create and embrace a better reality). In this case, the reality that gets blotted out is the real self. In our wishes and efforts to be ideal, we try to pretend the real self with its strengths *and* weaknesses does not exist.

Wishes to be ideal typically originate in childhood, when being ideal is the only way a shamed person knows how to establish connection with her parents. According to the parents' own slant on life, *ideal* might have many different meanings. It may mean *lawyer, doctor, never angry, perfectly polite,* or even *clever at deceiving.* We believe we have to perform—to live up to these definitions of ideal—in order to merit closeness with the significant people in our lives. We fervently wish for closeness that we're not getting with our parents, and we pretend if we were only more ideal, we would finally be close to them. Of course, acting a certain way to earn closeness precludes closeness. True closeness comes from being known and accepted as we are. But as children, this earned closeness may be the only connection we know to aim for, and we are left on a treadmill of always trying harder for an impossibly ideal self in order to obtain the longed-for connection.

This type of early childhood background leads to the continued adult pursuit of unrealistic perfection, such as what we saw happening in the lives of the pastor and the pianist. Neither of them acknowledged the honestly good performances they had delivered. They were so wrapped up in their wishes to be ideal that they could not acknowledge the fine performances made by their imperfect (but talented) selves. For the pianist and the pastor, it had to be a perfect performance, or it simply didn't count.

This brings us to the third self of the shame experience—the all-bad self. The all-bad self is made of the hurtful statements we make about ourselves over perceived failures as well as the painful feelings of unworthiness or inferiority triggered by these self-statements. The all-bad self is the self that stews in feelings of worthlessness, failure, and inferiority. Through statements such as "I can't believe I blew it!" "I hate myself," "When am I going to get it right?" and "I am so worthless," the shamed person punishes him or herself for not having lived up to the wish for perfection. This was the predicament of the pianist backstage after her concert and of the pastor in his study the day after the sermon. They berated themselves, wiping out their very good performances through negative self-statements that made both themselves and the particular performances in question *all bad*.

These negative self-statements feel awful, and they are the essence of low self-esteem. We feel unworthy, inferior, all bad, uniquely defective, outside the club of humanity, and uniquely broken in a world where everyone else seems to have it all together.

But the shame experience is not produced by the all-bad self in isolation. It is produced by an interplay of all three selves, and behind the low self-esteem of the all-bad self is always the high (*too* high) self-esteem of the all-good (ideal) self. In essence, we wish to be ideal, so we deny our real weaknesses and vulnerabilities through beating ourselves up as though the weakness and vulnerability should not exist. For example, in their hopes to be ideal, the pianist and the pastor cancel out their real performances which were actually very good. In this way, the real self is also blotted out over time. The real self—with its imperfect but very good performance—comes to be completely discounted in the quest for the ideal, even though the real self is the only self we can ever have or be.

Graphically, it might look like this:

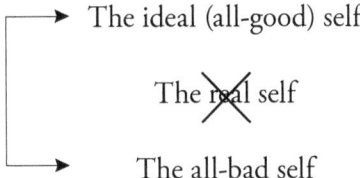

The ideal (all-good) self

The real self

The all-bad self

A Cost and a Benefit in Our Wish to Be Ideal

There is a bright side in our pursuit of an ideal self. It is the occasional, sublime *rush* when the wish is fulfilled—when it appears that the ideal self has been realized. Every now and then, the shamed person appears to have performed ideally or perfectly. Everything goes just right. He or she feels admired, and it is wonderful. The downside is that the person hangs in there through a lot of beatings for the rush. This rush of being admired and esteemed as ideal is all the person knows about well-being and feeling connected to others. But these feelings are not the same as being loved. Nonetheless, people caught up in this quest to be ideal find it comforting to believe that they can command admiration and thus ensure the only kind of closeness they have ever known. These rushes of good feelings over ideal performances ward off a deeper sadness and emptiness they have tried to avoid at all costs. This is the sadness and emptiness they felt when their parents overlooked aspects of their personalities. Their real selves were lost behind the performances their parents so admired.

The cost of pursuing the wish for an ideal self is very high. The cost is shame. Shame is one of the most traumatic emotions we experience. It is used in brainwashing because it can annihilate us in its severer forms. It can make us want to disappear deep inside ourselves. In its milder forms, it simply leaves us feeling painfully inadequate, perhaps hating ourselves, and perpetually striving to be good enough. Either way, it's a brutal bargain we strike when we endure the negative self-statements and feelings of unworthiness told to us by an all-bad self so that we can achieve a few highly rewarding moments of idealness.

One author talks about the "endless sequence"[5] to shame—about how our efforts to avoid shame dig us deeper and deeper into the very shame we are trying to avoid. This is exactly how our defensive wishing works. We strive after idealness in an effort to avoid shame, but it is our striving that creates and maintains shame.

The endless sequence seems hopeless, and in a sense it is. But this hopelessness is not necessarily bad. Unless we reach a point of despair, we will probably go right on clinging to the wishes that are not coming true and the depression, bitterness, and shame that go with them. This point of despair is what the alcoholic calls "bottoming out." It is essential to the alcoholic's recovery, and it is essential to the human being's growth.

It is very hard to let go of wishes. The resolution to shame involves mourning the loss of a deeply wished-for *wonder self*. But being at the point of despair—at our wit's end—can open our hearts and minds to new questions and to new answers. Despair can open us to mourning, letting go, and trying life from new angles.

Section 3 is about mourning, letting go, and trying life from new angles. It is about working through the dead-end wishes that have not come true. It is about being free to embrace real life.

SECTION 3
WISHING, MOURNING, AND JOY

CHAPTER 10

JOY IN THE MOURNING

In *The Great Divorce*, C. S. Lewis provides a winsome analogy that illustrates how enticing our illusions (false wishes) can be as well as how difficult but necessary it is to mourn and let go of them in order to be ultimately happy. The plot of Lewis's story centers around ghosts from hell taking a bus ride to heaven. These ghosts have invested their lives in illusions—in wishes that did not come true. Therefore, the ghosts lack substance; they are mere shadows. On the bus ride, one ghost talks to a peer, describing the ghosts' way of life in hell:

"They have no needs. You get everything you want (not very good quality, of course) by just imagining it. That's why it never costs any trouble to move to another street or build another house."[1] The ghost is describing the rich allure of a fantasy world—of the seeming power and gratification we feel when we allow ourselves to get absorbed in pursuing unrealistic wishes.

But even the ghost from hell realizes there is a cost to these unrealistic wishes and senses that reality may be more desirable than illusion. He tells his peer of plans to get "*real* commodities"[2] when they visit heaven and then market these real commodities in hell.

His cohort responds, "But look here…if they can get everything just by imagining it, why would they want any REAL things, as you call them?"[3]

The first ghost explains, "Eh? Oh well, they'd like houses that really kept out the rain."[4] Thus, at some level, even the ghosts sense that their illusions do not satisfy, and they seek reality.

Pursuing reality is costly as can be seen when the ghosts arrive at heaven, where they encounter the solid people who inhabit heaven. One of these solid beings tries to persuade one of the ghosts to stay in heaven.

Knowing that the ghost would ultimately be happier if he would enter heaven but also that trading in hell for heaven would involve a painful process, the solid being says, "Will you come with me to the mountains? It will hurt at first, until your feet are hardened. Reality is harsh to the feet of shadows. But will you come?"[5]

The ghost refuses. Heaven's grass is "hard as diamonds" to his "unsubstantial feet."[6] It seems to the ghost that entering this unaccustomed realm of reality simply hurts too much. So he stays with his illusions.

Like the ghosts, we all face the dilemma of whether or not to let go of our unrealistic wishes. We have a choice between reality and illusion, but reality *is* harsh to the feet of shadows. Suffering the sadness of letting go of our illusions is the necessary pathway to becoming more solidly grounded in reality—to pursuing real relationships, building real houses, or having real careers—all of which, though flawed and limited, can deeply satisfy us and lead us to profound joy.

This painful process of trading in our illusions for reality is the process behind gaining wisdom. Literature on the subject of wisdom teaches that wisdom is a source of joy or well-being. But there is a seeming contradiction in the descriptions of wisdom found in Proverbs and Ecclesiastes. Proverbs 3:13-15 says it is of great value, better than anything you could desire. Ecclesiastes 1:18, however, says that much wisdom increases grief. Paradoxically, both statements are true. This is what C. S. Lewis's *solid* person is trying to communicate to the ghost when he encourages him to go through the painful process of entering heaven. Reality is wondrous, but the process of becoming real is quite painful. Reality is indeed harsh to the feet of the shadows.

The fact is that wisdom, being in tune with reality, is acquired only through the painful process of mourning the loss of our unrealistic wishes. There must be a transition from defensive or unrealistic wishing to healthy wishing. We must be willing to mourn and let go of our defensive wishes in order to pursue our own realistic wishes. Letting go of our unrealistic wishes and dreams *is* a harsh and painful process. But the well-being that comes from being grounded in reality and pursuing realistic wishes and dreams is ultimately well worth the pain.

A Restoration Process

Working our way through the layers of our defensive wishes and back to our *nephesh* (soul) can be quite an excavation project, but as a memorable experience illustrates, the end result is worth the effort.

C. S. Lewis is one of my heroes, and I had the privilege of working with the C. S. Lewis Foundation[7] on the restoration of his home, the Kilns, in Oxford, England. When the work team first arrived at the Kilns, the place was so overgrown with vines and brush that the home could not even be seen from the street. As rain poured down on us, we started pulling and hacking away at the overgrowth. There could be no orderly approach. We had to pull and hack just to be able to see what we were pulling. After the fact, we realized we had pulled ivy off a fence so old and rotted that it needed the vines to support it.

A skilled landscaper was overseeing the project, and a brilliantly conceived master plan had been devised, computerized, laminated, and hung on one of the walls of the house. Despite these carefully developed plans, the restoration project was often a chaotic mess.

Much of the time, we were formulating plans as we went along. It felt messy, discouraging, and even hopeless since sometimes we had to undo what we had just done. We worked hard at tedious tasks we weren't sure were necessary. We hung in there and kept plugging along. It was not always clear what the end of the project would be like, and the work wasn't always fun. It's hard to keep the vision when you are overwhelmed by muck and details. After a while, though, the original plan became a reality. Amazingly, the team had transformed the Kilns into a charming home.

So it is when we set about to restore our souls. Souls need to be excavated from the debris of defensive wishes. The restoration project gets messy and chaotic, and at times, it seems endless. As we pull *weeds*, often frenetically, we sometimes unwittingly uproot the good growth with the bad. The layers of debris can seem never-ending. We unearth the depression, bitterness, and shame created by pursuing unrealistic wishes—the wishes and feelings we developed to defend ourselves against the barrenness left by the splitting and spoiling in our souls. In turn, the splitting and spoiling protected us from little-boy and little-girl hurts that were just too big to deal with at the time. With so much overgrowth, we can't even begin to see our soul from the road. In fact, sometimes we wonder if it's really there at all. We lose our vision in the confusion. But there is a soul in there, and it can be restored just as Daniel's story powerfully illustrates.

A Story of Wishing, Mourning, and Joy

At the age of three, Daniel's world was abruptly turned upside down. His father divorced his mother, trading her in for a new model—a vivacious, opinionated, career-oriented woman who stood in stark contrast to Daniel's timid, cowering, highly apologetic mother. Because Daniel's mother could not negotiate well in the world, let alone in the court system, Daniel's father managed to get custody of Daniel. His father loved Daniel. However, in his new marriage relationship, Daniel's father found himself in a classic role reversal. The father was now the milquetoast partner, while the stepmother was strong, compelling, in charge, and *mean*. In this new relationship, Daniel's father didn't dare set any limits on his wife. Consequently, there was no one to protect the young boy from her meanness.

In group therapy one day, Daniel was dealing with childhood losses that had begun with all this trauma. Using a group therapy technique called psychodrama, I guided Daniel and the group members (with different peers playing the roles of members of Daniel's family) in acting out some of the events of Daniel's trauma in order to get a clearer perspective on them. Daniel's occasional escape from his dominating stepmother had been the sporadic visits of his birth mother. We played out a visit with her. Especially touching were Daniel's last moments he would spend with her in the car. She would tell him how much she loved him. When he got out, he would stand at the edge of the road until she disappeared out of sight. Slowly, he would turn away to once again face the place where he lived. With all his strength, he would try to quell the overwhelming sadness and conjure up the courage he needed before he reentered the world of his stepmother.

Daniel allowed himself to face this sadness and then talked more about his early experiences. His stepmother would sometimes do the one thing he hated most—lock him in a very dark closet. He tried to avoid being locked in the closet, but he never knew exactly what he did to cause him to be locked up. He did always know by the look on her face that it was coming. This was abuse—abuse without visible bruises or scars, abuse without wounds to show anyone had he tried to tell people what was happening to him. But Daniel didn't try to tell anyone. He sensed that neither his father nor his mother was strong enough to protect him.

So in our group therapy session, Daniel asked someone to play the role of him as a little boy. He recreated the closet scene. In this scene, his stepmother locked him in the closet and then walked away with a pleased grin on her face. The one who was acting as Daniel shouted, pleaded, and pounded on the door in terror. As Daniel watched all of this unfold, he uttered, "How can she enjoy a little guy's terror? I want to protect that little boy!"

So as the therapist, I gave Daniel permission to go back in time and do whatever he needed to do to protect that little boy. A very interesting thing happened. Daniel chose the role of a policeman who happened to be walking by and heard the little boy's cries. Daniel, playing the part of the policeman, was just about to intervene. His hand was raised to knock on the door, and the stepmother was about to be apprehended when all of a sudden, Daniel simply shrunk back and said, "I can't do this." For a moment, he was given the power to rewrite the script—to overcome the stepmother and rescue the little boy. But he could not do it. *Why?*

All his life a little boy's wish had stopped Daniel from exercising power. That same wish was blocking him now from rewriting his history. He had hung on to the wish tenaciously because it had helped him escape from an intolerable living situation. A mean stepmother had replaced a loving mother. That reality was simply more than he could bear, so he had created a bright fantasy world. In this imaginary world, when Daniel's stepmother said or did cruel things to him, his mother would unexpectedly appear. Appalled and indignant, she would silence the stepmother and whisk Daniel away to comfort him with kind, loving words. It was a *happily ever after* fantasy. This fantasy was a wonderful, much-needed form of self-soothing. Morning after morning it gave him the hope and the *oomph* he needed to get out of bed and enter a dreadful situation.

The problem unraveled like this: A little boy who is abused is the only one who gets this magic mommy to swoop in and rescue him. If he grows up and casts off his abuser—if he uses his own resources and works through the pain of his abuse—the need for a magic mother disappears. Daniel couldn't bear to lose his fantasy mother, so he stayed in this abused little-boy posture long into adulthood. In the group role-play, he could not apply the storybook power given him because if he overcame his stepmother, his magic mother would never need to come.

As an adult, his choices to stay a little boy were subtle. He never said no to anyone. He agreed with everyone else's opinions. He was easily wounded, even by comments that weren't addressed to him. He came across as a very weak, very damaged person. People often swooped in to rescue his hurt feelings or to reassure him that they liked him. But they would feel strangely stifled by and frustrated with Daniel. People soon gave up pursuing serious friendships with him.

We had uncovered the defensive wish. Now we would act out another scene to get a better perspective on it. Daniel instructed a peer to portray his ideal mother as decisive, strong, assertive, and highly committed to her little boy. This mother was exquisite; she left the abusive stepmother quivering in fear as the whole fantasy rescue scene was played out in the psychodrama. Daniel saw and felt it all—the vicarious, soul-deep thrill of having his mother rally to the defense of her little boy. This indeed had been one of Daniel's deepest wishes. But now as Daniel began to realize the cost of the wish, he wanted to let go of it. He did not like being *stuck* in a cowering position before an abusive stepmother, and, therefore, cowering before the whole world as well.

In our group psychodrama, we left Daniel's ideal mom, the little Daniel, and the now cowering stepmother right where they were and set up another scene right beside the first. The second scene was of Daniel's mother as he actually remembered her—a weak, unassertive woman who required caretaking from a three-year-old boy. As Daniel looked on and clearly saw the wished-for mom side by side with a weak, less idealized version of his mother, reality began to sink in. He realized he had never had what he really wanted from his biological mother. In that moment he did some sober growing up.

How is it that Daniel did not realize before this moment that he had never gotten what he wanted? His whole childhood was about not getting it. Every day was another painful reminder. But he had never really come to grips with his disappointments in his mother. By continuing to wish, he was able to ward off a too painful reality. By still holding out for the wish to come true—just around the corner—he could deny the reality of what was happening.

When the scene was finished, Daniel went over and shook hands with the wished-for mom. He told her that he had always thought it would be so wonderful to meet her but that this was a sad moment for him. He was at last meeting her, and at the same time, he needed to say goodbye. He told her she was everything he had ever wanted, except she wasn't real. Daniel went through an eloquent, heartfelt, sad, and courageous goodbye to her. Daniel wanted houses that could keep the rain out.

CHAPTER 11

BEHIND THE SCENES OF A HAPPY ENDING

When I was a child, Sunday nights meant two things to me—family night and great TV. My father really enjoyed Westerns, and I have very warm memories of watching *Bonanza* with him. It was during this time that I fell in love with Michael Landon (also known as Little Joe). Even though he's gone from us, I still love Michael Landon. And so I was watching *Little House on the Prairie* the other day and saw a touching illustration of people letting go of wishes and taking steps through the mourning process.

Half-Pint was asking Ma and Pa what they would wish for if they could have anything in the world they wanted. With a little prodding, Pa said he would want a bigger house with separate rooms for his daughters and a room for Ma's sewing. Ma said she would want money to be able to go to Mrs. Olson's store and buy anything she wanted. This illustrates the *first step* to letting go of our unrealistic wishes—simply putting our wishes clearly into words.

Then Half-Pint and a buddy discovered gold. Half-Pint was *very* excited. She had a wish of her own--to be able to give her mom and dad what they wanted in life. Secretly, she and her buddy panned for gold; she would sneak off from school to pursue her dream. In exchange for her buddy's help, Half-Pint gave him one of her most precious possessions. This leads to the *second step* of letting go of our wishes—counting the cost of continuing to pursue the wish. Half-Pint's wish cost her time, effort, and a prized possession, but in spite of what it was costing her, Half-Pint was caught up in pursuing her wish.

Expectantly, she took her gold to the town banker. Sensitively, protectively, he told her it wasn't worth anything. He hesitated before using the term "fool's gold." Then he said a very wise and kind thing. He said, "It's the worst kind of hurt to want something so badly you hardly even dare to dream it will come true…and then to not get it." In taking her gold to the banker and listening to his feedback, Half-Pint (perhaps unwittingly!) was fulfilling the *third and fourth steps* to letting go of our wishes—subjecting our wishes to reality-testing and making a choice to let go of them.

It hurt badly. Half-Pint was very sad. She had been caught up in her dreams. But now she was mourning and letting go of her wishes. The banker let her father know what had happened.

Enter Pa to help her through the sadness. Half-Pint lamented to him that she had hoped and dreamed and worked at getting the gold because she was going to give him and Ma everything they had ever wanted—the big house and the goods from Mrs. Olson's store. It had all seemed so wonderful, but none of it was going to happen. This illustrates the *fifth step* of letting go of our unrealistic wishes— that is, facing a momentary despair about them as we realize they are not going to come true. This is where the most intense mourning begins, and it is noteworthy that at this point Half-Pint had a wise comforter in her father. Comforters are essential in the process of coming to grips with the sadness of our lost wishes.

But there is still another step in mourning and letting go of our wishes. When Pa said, "Half-Pint, you give us everything we want every day of our lives. You give us love and respect and joy…" Pa was letting Half-Pint know that the reality of what he already had far exceeded any wishes and dreams he might have. This is the *final step* of mourning and letting go of our wishes. In this step our passions are invited back from the unrealistic wishes to be invested in real loves. Although he could fantasize about a better life, Pa's passions were solidly invested in the here and now of his real family. He drew great satisfaction and joy from this, his real world. And Half-Pint, too, could draw great satisfaction and joy from this real world where she already fulfilled her father's wishes just by being who she was.

Letting go of wishes that aren't coming true is a mourning process. And when we finally let go, the result is a freeing up of our passions so that we can invest them in reality and know the joy of wishes that *do* come true.

The steps of the mourning process are

1. putting the wish into words,
2. confronting the cost of the wish,
3. introducing the wish to reality,
4. making a choice,
5. facing a momentary despair, and
6. freeing up our passions to reinvest in realistic wishes.

Daniel's Process Revisited

We find these steps in Daniel's story as well. The steps are less orderly and more complex than on TV, but there are happy endings in real life too. As in Half-Pint's story, Daniel, too, had to give up his wishes and walk through sadness in order to get to the happy ending. Let's look at an in-depth analysis of the steps to Daniel's mourning.

Step 1: Putting the wish into words

Putting our wishes into words seems like an odd and unnecessary step. It seems like we would already know our wishes. But we typically don't have words for our most deep-seated and therefore most compelling wishes. This was certainly true of Daniel. His wish for a strong, ideal mother was his strongest, most central desire and the driving motivation of his life. Yet it was unconscious.

As he grew up, Daniel had put his wish out of his mind to protect himself from the shame and disappointment of longing intensely for his mother when the wish was so rarely gratified. But putting things out of our minds can actually increase their power. The buried wish had lived on as the driving motivation of his life. In order for Daniel to mourn and let go of the wish, he would first have to uncover it and put it into words. Although there were definite clues that a wish for an ideal mother existed, his wish was a wordless, undefined, but compelling longing.

So it is with all of us. Our most driving wishes are often unconscious. Therefore, it is important to know the clues that point to our having wishes. There are typically two major clues to unrealistic wishes.

The first clue includes our mood. When we suffer depression, bitterness, or shame, it is often a clue that we are caught up in the pursuit of unrealistic wishes. Depression, bitterness, and shame were certainly the first indicators that something really was wrong in Daniel's life. That *something* would turn out to be an unconscious wish for an ideal mother being played out in hurtful ways.

The second clue to unconscious wishes involves our behavior. In Daniel's case, he was engaging in certain compulsive behaviors. For Daniel and for all of us, our unconscious wishes come out masked as strong compulsions—irresistible urges to do something that is against what we consciously will. The strength of the desire of our unconscious wishes plus the fact that we are not aware of them combine to give these wishes a seemingly irresistible power over us.

Unconscious wishes keep manifesting themselves in seemingly irrational, self-sabotaging behaviors. Compulsions may come out as sexual promiscuity, overeating, workaholism, alcoholism—all the addictions we hear about so often. But the common thread behind all these different addictions is the sense that our behavior is out of control. It is like the apostle Paul's infamous dilemma. "For that which I am doing, I do not understand; for I am not practicing what I would like to do, but I am doing the very thing I hate" (Rom 7:15). Our behavior seems irrational and self-sabotaging because it is against what we consciously want. It seems as though there is someone else inside us making us do these things. But it's not someone else. It's a hidden part of ourselves, buried desires that we have pushed out of our awareness.

Daniel's compulsion was not a classic addiction. Rather it was under assertiveness. Daniel had a major contradiction between the way he consciously wanted to behave and the way he actually behaved regarding self-assertion. Daniel wanted to be a strong, confident, stereotypically manly guy. But he found himself coming across to others in a weak and self-effacing manner. All of this didn't make sense until we discovered Daniel's unconscious wish to be rescued by a strong mother. Only weak little boys need rescuing by strong mothers. When this wish came to light, Daniel's wimpy way of relating to people made perfect sense for the first time.

It is important to note that as Daniel uncovered what it was he really longed for, the wishes didn't just involve the here and now. They were expressed in the present but were also rooted in the past. And so it is with most of us. Our core wishes involve a connection with the past. Our wishes will usually involve a fantasy or ideal mother or father. The fantasy may have been played out with many different people in the past and present such as aunts, uncles, older siblings, spouses, or friends. But it almost always involves what we deeply wanted as children in our interactions with our significant caretakers.

Putting the wish into words is not an overnight project. It requires time, time, and more time. We bury our wishes deeply to protect them from exposure—from the humiliation of realizing we want something we cannot have. But once we embrace the wish, we will know it by the intense longing we feel. It's the kind of longing that brings tears to our eyes. There may also be a sense of "Yes! That's it! That's what I've been wanting my whole life!" Putting the wish into words involves both uncovering the specific content of the wish and uncovering the deep longings that go with the wish.

Step 2: Confronting the cost of the wish

We could also call this step doing a cost-benefit analysis of the wish. Daniel did this. The benefit of Daniel's wishing as a child was that it gave him hope in a desperate situation. The benefit as an adult was that from time to time when someone would appear to gratify his magic mommy wish, it felt pretty wonderful. And it would, after all, be thrilling *if* his wish were to come true tomorrow and Daniel were to get the ideal mother figure he had always wanted. It certainly seemed to Daniel that this would finally make up for his deprived childhood. Daydreaming about having his wish fulfilled caused Daniel to feel a sublime, hopeful feeling. The wish had become its own reward. It felt good while he believed in it.

The cost of holding on to his wish was that it maintained three layers of pain in him. They were

- the original deep sadness about a mother who was not there for him and a stepmother who was mean rather than loving,
- the pain of the repeated disappointments when the magic mother never quite materialized, and
- the pain of the lost adulthood and adult-to-adult friendships Daniel could not have until he gave up his posture of being a cowering little boy waiting for a mom to rescue him.

Part of the problem in doing a cost-benefit analysis like this is that once we realize how much it is costing us, the wonder of the wish automatically lessens. Daniel had not realized what he was wishing or what it was costing him. He had been on automatic pilot, reflexively acting out unresolved issues from childhood. As he realized exactly what he wanted and what the pursuit of his wish was costing him, he began to want it less. He was already introducing his wish to reality.

Step 3: Introducing the wish to reality

A profound thing happens when a wish meets reality. It may seem like a happy thing—an occasion to celebrate. It is, but it is a happiness mixed with sadness.

Daniel was introducing his wish to reality when he represented his wished-for mother beside a weaker version of his mother in the psychodrama. This happened in two steps. First, he acted out the scene with his wished-for mother and let himself experience all the deep longing he had had for this wonder woman and the thrill of finally meeting her. (This was actually part of step one, putting his wish into words.) Then—and this was the terribly courageous part—he acted out the scene with his mother as he remembered her, weak and unassertive. In this step Daniel was putting his wish side by side with reality. As he saw the real weaknesses of his mother beside his wished-for mother, the sad reality began to sink in. The wished-for mother would never be. He was mourning.

But if reality is to sink in, Daniel will need to introduce his wish to reality many times. Our wishes are tenacious. They are masters of rationalization, of wheeling and dealing, and of making black seem white. Our longings will clamor to be believed and acted on, and if we are to transform them into realistic longings, we must confront our unrealistic wishes with reality again and again.

The reality statements we make—like Daniel's picture of his mother as he remembered her in contrast with his wished-for mother—are perspectives we figure out in our clearer moments. Because wishes can muddy our thinking, we will need to think through our reality statements in moments when we are not caught up too intensely in our longings.

Our reality statements will be tailored to our specific wishes. For example, we may need to address our longing for certain romantic partners with the reality of telltale signs that those partners don't really care for us as much as we wish they did. Or perhaps we are about to embark on a shopping spree. We revel in the thought of all the new possessions (clothes, expensive tools, video games, accessories...) we will enjoy, but we subject our reveling to the reality of our budget, of how it feels to be enslaved to a credit card, and of how it would feel to have no option to buy new things next year because we are saddled to this debt. Or we may need to address our longings for food with the reality that we don't fit into our clothes. Besides, we are really longing for other things that the food does not begin to satisfy. (The reality statements may get complex as we begin to address deeper wishes hidden behind surface wishes.)

Whatever the specific wishes, a reality statement includes exactly what it is we wish, the cost of pursuing it, and the signs we see that the wish probably will not come true. The statement should be detailed, heartfelt, and perhaps thought through with the help of friends. It may be helpful to actually write down our reality statements—as a kind of creed to turn to whenever we are about to regress into the pursuit of wishes that aren't going to come true.

Step 4: Making a choice

The point of reality-testing our wishes is to reach a decision about whether to go on pursuing them or to mourn and let go of them. Daniel defined his wish, saw what pursuing the wish was costing him, and decided the wish was unrealistic. He came to see that he wished for an ideal mother—a strong woman dedicated to meeting all his needs; that the wish was costing him adult freedom, mature friendships, and liberation from an ongoing depression; and that after thirty-some years of futile searching, the fantasy woman probably did not exist.

Having gained this awareness, Daniel still needed to decide whether or not to keep pursuing his wish. To us the choice may seem obvious. But only Daniel could make that choice. And so it is with all of us. Even as we realize the high costs of seemingly unattainable wishes, we still have to make a choice. All of us need to decide for ourselves what is illusion and what is reality. We have to decide where we want to place our energies.

It often happens that people choose to pursue wishes that other people judge to be foolish and a waste of time—and the wishes do come true. The Jewish patriarch Abraham believed fervently for years and years in an impossibility. He waited for a son that God had promised him. He wished for this son even after he was too old to reproduce and Sarah, his wife, had gone through menopause. Against all odds, Abraham's wish came true, and Isaac was born.

On the other hand, people choose to let go of fervent wishes that others may think they should keep pursuing. The apostle Paul wished for the removal of a thorn in his flesh and prayed three times to that end. Miraculous healings were happening quite frequently. Paul himself had been miraculously healed at least twice. Perhaps some people hated for Paul to give up his wish. Perhaps they thought if only he prayed a little harder or believed a little more strongly, he would reap the rewards then. But God told him to stop praying, that it would not be removed. Paul gave up on his wish, and with a singular focus, he reinvested his desires in other things.

Each of these men had to weigh the data available and then make a highly individualized choice. Usually, we don't get such clear statements from God about our particular wishes. Perhaps even Abraham and Paul wondered at times if they had heard God correctly! But we, too, need to take responsibility for weighing the data and choosing which wishes to pursue and which to let go of. Even when we think we have heard God's voice regarding cherished wishes, we need to take responsibility for discerning (often with outside help) whether *it really was the voice of God.* Or was it the voice of an idealized friend that sometimes gets confused with God? Or was it my own fervent wishes disguising themselves compellingly as the voice of God?

The act of *choosing*—which implies we take responsibility for making our own choices and for the outcomes—can be extremely difficult. We try to avoid choosing. We try to turn our choices over to someone else.

A Christian wife, torn between conflicting wishes, tried to turn her choice over to her husband. She believed she was submitting to him according to biblical standards. Wisely, her husband said, "Honey, I can't tell you what you want." He left her in the struggle to discern her own wishes. He also entered into the struggle with her, asking her questions that would help her to clarify her deepest longings.

Many of us, like this wife, try to turn our decisions over to so-called authority figures. It may be a pastor, a therapist, or simply an authoritative friend who is all too willing to give advice. Certainly, there *are* times when we (women *and* men) give up our choices out of a motive of godly submission or for the greater welfare. Often, however, we try to get other people to make our decisions for us in order to avoid personal responsibility for our choices and their outcomes. We want to avoid the risks and unknowns of choosing, especially when our choices are those loaded choices regarding our deepest wishes. There is just too much at stake. We want to know the *right* choice with the guaranteed outcome. (And we also want someone else to blame for our failed outcomes!)

But in this business of choosing among our wishes, there is usually no right or wrong choice—no perfect choice. There is only trying to accurately read our own souls and our God. If we choose to stop pursuing a wish, there will be gains and losses. If we choose to keep pursuing a wish, there will be gains and losses. When we take responsibility for choosing, we assess the relative gains and losses and make the best choices we can on limited data. (As we make our choices, there is also no hindsight—not yet. We will probably regret some of our choices.)

This is the freedom and tension of adulthood. As adults, we no longer have parents who can figure out the right choices for us.

Only we have the power to discern and choose what we truly want in life. We may consult with respected, objective friends or experts. We should research certain choices carefully. Certainly, we may need to take others into account in our choices. But we make our choices, and we have no one else to blame for the outcomes.

When we give our power to choose to other people as though they know what we truly want in life better than we do, we are again pursuing the wish for magic parents. And that's really okay. I am not condemning anyone in their quest for a perfect parent. (Perhaps that very universal longing is a manifestation of our spirits searching for God.) I am saying that we need to know our wishes and what they are costing us, and make a conscious rather than an unconscious choice about pursuing them.

But there is a paradox here. Once we begin to face and understand the wishes of childhood—and to take responsibility for our adult choices—we have already begun to grow up, even if we choose to stay children.

Step 5: Facing a momentary despair

The wishes we are mourning and letting go of are deep wishes. They are not the simple wishes we made as children when looking at the first star of the night or throwing a coin into a well. They are consuming wishes. They are life wishes that have been the secret motivation of our lives.

When we persistently confront these deep soul wishes with reality, we reach a point of hopelessness—a temporary but very real despair. This despair is not a bad thing. In fact, we must despair of—give up on—these wishes if we are to let go of them. (When these wishes are our deepest longings, a little bit of sadness won't do the trick. We must *despair*.) Despair is a necessary step in the mourning process. It is also a momentary state we pass through. We can be sure it won't go on forever. But it *is* despair—an agonizingly painful feeling.

Daniel chose to walk through this despair. For Daniel, this despair meant confronting not only intense sadness but also emptiness. There was an empty space in his heart where once there had been a wonderful—though unreal—mother. He felt painfully alone.

There were moments when he wanted to turn back from the despair. In these moments he was sorely tempted to return to his unrealistic wishes. It seemed that if he could only slip back into his wish for an ideal parent for a moment, the pain would be anesthetized. When reality became this painful, his unrealistic wishes seemed far preferable; they seemed quite soothing.

But he had comforters in his corner—real people who were also willing to soothe him in his pain. With gentle reminders, "That was then; now can be different," they encouraged him to stay in the mourning process. He did.

He continued to hold the image of his wished-for mother and of his mother as he remembered her together in his heart. He continued to feel the deep longings for his fantasy mother, and he continued to face reality. He continued to feel deeply sad for a time.

This sadness was gut-wrenching. But it was not the same overwhelming, never-ending sadness he had needed to avoid in order to survive as a child. He was an adult now. Sometimes childhood sadness really is intended for just such a time as this—a time when, as adults, we have other resources and more mature understanding. Once we have faced the nightmare, we *can* wake from it.

So Daniel volunteered for his moment of despair. He committed to it and continued to walk through the mourning process in spite of how hard the feelings became. But as he continued to mourn and genuinely but firmly instruct his longings about the way things really were, his passions were slowly freed to invest in wishes that could come true.

Step 6: Freeing up our passions to reinvest in realistic wishes

There were at least two very bright spots for Daniel in the resolution process. First, as he faced his deep sadness, the group began to see the real person behind the manipulative defenses that had alienated him from others. For the first time, they began to feel a kinship with him. Group members did not demean his little-boy longings as those longings surfaced. Rather they were relieved to finally understand why he always took an inferior position with them. Now they could give Daniel grace for behavior that had formerly alienated them.

This is what understanding is all about. When they finally understood, they spontaneously gathered around Daniel to hug him, shake hands, and clap him on the back. Daniel was experiencing his first taste of being an adult among adults and a friend among friends. He liked it.

Daniel was experiencing community. He was also experiencing comfort as he and his peers began to understand his deep sadness. It's hard to say if the comfort of his peers enabled him to face his sadness or if facing his sadness enabled him to open up to his peers and be comforted. But looking back at Daniel's process, it was clear to all of us that the comfort we find in a community of people who witness our pain and also care that it happened is pivotal in facing and resolving our losses.

The second bright spot happened as Daniel was saying goodbye to his ideal mother. He began to orchestrate a third scene with his mother. The mother he was now creating was not an ideal mother. Nor was she merely a weak mother who couldn't meet Daniel's needs. She was a *real* mother whose genuine caring for her little boy had some serious flaws. Daniel gave the actress who played his real mother a heartfelt hug. At last, he was beginning to accept his mother for who she really was.

How did this happen? As Daniel let go of his wishes for an ideal mother, he began to take back his own power to live life as a free adult, and his attitude toward his real mother began to change. He no longer held her accountable for his welfare. He began to be able to see her simply as a fellow member in this club of adults. As he saw her in this manner, he was able to maintain warm feelings about a stumbling, hurting human being who had tried and failed, tried and succeeded, tried and failed in her long-ago efforts to mother him. He was at last able to embrace the efforts, failures, successes, and pain of a real mother.

Daniel was embracing his real mother. Don't miss the importance of this. When we hang onto wishes for ideal mothers or ideal fathers, we crave things we cannot have. A real parent cannot live up to the image of a fantasy parent. So disappointment in the real parent is magnified; she or he may be written off as all bad. Thus, we blot out our real parents in our quest for ideal parents, and this creates holes and emptiness in our own souls. But accepting our real parents—honoring them for who they are with the good and the bad—creates well-being (See Eph 6:2, 3). Daniel was on the road to well-being at last.

CHAPTER 12

THE END OF SHAME: LETTING GO OF THE WISH FOR AN IDEAL SELF

In letting go of a wish, the wish always needs to be confronted with reality. Similarly, in the resolution of shame, our wish for ideal selves needs to be confronted by our real selves. This happened in the cases of two famous biblical characters—the apostle Peter and King David. In the course of their lives, Peter and David were both humbled. They were starkly confronted with the reality of who they were. When they saw who they were, they were able to give up their idealized views of themselves.

The apostle Peter became aware of his inflated view of himself one night after a dialogue with Christ. Christ said to his disciples, "You will all fall away because of me this night." Christ further cited prophetic scripture to support his prediction. "For it is written, 'I will strike down the shepherd, and the sheep of the flock shall be scattered'" (Mt 26:31). Because the disciples were growing in their awareness of Christ's deity, we might have expected they would believe him. But in his unbridled wish to be ideal, Peter responded,

"*Even* though all may fall away because of You, I will never fall away" (Mt 26:33). Then Jesus told Peter he would deny him three times before the cock crowed. Peter asserted his ideal self—the self he wished he were—even more emphatically. "Even if I have to die with You, I will not deny You" (Mt 26:35). Peter was making incredibly forthright statements about his wish to be ideal. (You and I often mask our wishes to be ideal so that they are not quite so obvious.) Peter wanted to be the sort of man who would be loyal to Christ to the very end. But Jesus was seeing Peter differently than Peter saw himself.

Peter needed to get a more realistic view of himself. It happened through a series of events. As predicted, Peter denied Jesus three times during the course of the night. In a desperate attempt to convince accusers that he was not a companion of Christ, he even laced his third denial with cursing and swearing. Very significantly, after the third denial, "immediately a cock crowed" (Mt 26:74).

Jesus knew how tenaciously we hang on to our wishes to be ideal—even in the face of staggering evidence to the contrary. So he gave Peter a very specific cue, and when Peter heard the cock crow, it clicked in his mind. He "remembered the word which Jesus had said" (Mt 26:75) and had to deal with his unrealistic wishes to be ideal. He realized he *had* denied Christ. He had failed to live up to his own ideal. In that instant, real self met ideal self, and Peter wept—for his betrayal of Jesus and for the loss of the ideal self he had so wished to be. Peter had to accept the reality of his flawed and sinful self.

King David was another man who believed passionately in God yet proudly wished to be ideal. He continued wishing until he sinned and lost his idealistic view of himself. It wasn't until his fall that he came to understand who he was before God. David's image of himself as ideal became clear when he overstepped marital boundaries to have sex with Bathsheba, and it was even clearer when he overstepped the ultimate boundary and had Bathsheba's husband killed. This behavior was clearly not ideal, but he was blind to his own sinfulness. His behavior demonstrated what may be called a *grandiose self*—a specific type of ideal self. In David's particular distorted wish to be ideal, he saw himself as larger than life and above the law. He was acting as though he were a special case and not subject to the constraints that limit other mortals.

Like Peter, King David needed to have an encounter between his real self and his ideal self. God orchestrated this encounter through Nathan the prophet.

Nathan told David a story about a poor man who "had nothing except one little ewe lamb which he bought and nourished; and it grew up together with him and his children...and was like a daughter to him" (2 Sm 12:3). Then a rich man who had no lack of resources took the little lamb from the poor man and prepared it for a visiting traveler. Nathan asked, "What should be done with the rich man?"

David's response to Nathan's parable revealed how much his wish to be ideal had distorted his self-image. Even in the face of the sins he had just committed and the blatant parallel between himself and the rich man of the story, he had no inkling that the story was about him. Rather scripture says, "Then David's anger burned greatly against the man..." *This awful man, so different from decent people like me,* David must have thought. *Who could do such a thing?* "...and he said to Nathan, 'As the Lord lives, surely the man who has done this deserves to die'" (2 Sm 12:5).

Nathan's response must have come as a shock to David. "You are the man" (v. 7). As was true with both Peter and David, it always comes as a shock to us to realize we are not as ideal as we had hoped we were. It is devastating to reckon with our own badness and acknowledge that "I am the man!" So instead we get indignant about other people's evilness. It's easier to dwell in shocked horror on the cruelty of a Hitler, a Hussein, or some other evil person than to admit that "I am the man!" The idea of "I am the man" is hard for all of us to accept because that statement is at the core of a meeting between our ideal and our real selves.

I sometimes do an exercise in group therapy to communicate this truth to clients. I have them brainstorm about the most awful type of person they know. It usually turns out to be a rapist or child molester. Then some brave soul stands in the middle of the room to represent the bad guy, and the group heaps venom upon him or her. Most of the clients have been victimized in some way and are finally able to get angry about their abuse. So in this role-playing situation, a lot of righteous indignation and years of heaped-up hostility come gushing out against this person who volunteered to role-play the bad guy. Group members experience tremendous relief and a sense of communion as they share in berating the enemy.

Then I throw a difficult twist into the exercise. After the venom is somewhat spent, I instruct people to embrace this man as though he were themselves. I ask them to reach out to him in a way that shows communion with him and to thus acknowledge the parts of themselves that have also victimized others. I ask them to acknowledge their less-than-ideal selves through identifying with this bad guy. Some may not be ready for this, especially those who have just begun to realize their abusers were wrong and what happened was not their fault. Like the abused woman in the movie *Forrest Gump*, some simply need to throw stones at their homes and to get fiercely angry at the abuser for a time as they realize the undeserved awfulness of what happened to them. But others are ready for the exercise and are even relieved to own the parts of themselves that have hurt others.

One woman gave a hearty hug to the role-player and then confessed to secret, murderous fantasies she had about her male coworkers. She had been enraged by the way she and other women were always passed over for promotion. Grossly unfair, it felt just like growing up with a favored brother. Another woman shook hands with the role player and gleefully told him how she had secretly sabotaged her male bosses by putting deliberate miscommunications in letters she sent out for them. These bosses had done nothing to her, but they were men in positions of authority over her. She said it felt good to see the tables turned after the years of sexual abuse she suffered as a child at the hands of a male teacher.

One man in the group stood arm in arm with the role-player and revealed how he had always felt so passive and demeaned in the presence of women. It had started with an overpowering mother. This man had become absolutely delighted by pornography, especially pornography that depicted women as disdainfully subjected to men. He was reluctant to admit how good it felt to finally get the last word in his power struggle with women.

In sharing these fantasies, it may sound like people were being frivolous about sin. They were not. They were struggling to own and confess their sins. It is difficult to convey the courage it takes for people to stand in front of other people who are also angry at abusers and say, "I am the man!" Those who are ready to participate in this part of the exercise do it with great hesitation and awkwardness. The fear of rejection is painfully evident on their faces. They are not taking their sinfulness lightly. Rather they are daring to come to grips with it.

In group therapy as in life, it is easy for the group to focus on the bad guys who are outside the group and thereby to avoid seeing the bad guys who are inside the group—the you and I, present here and now, who also do wrong. At times we envy one another, vie to be special, and wish bad things on one another. We also genuinely care for and support one another. But if group members see only the goodness in themselves and attribute wrongdoing only to people outside the group, the group members' individual wishes to be ideal are supported in grand style. It is only when I realize that *I* also do wrong—"*I* am the man"—that my ideal self is confronted by my real self. And it is only when that confrontation takes place that I am ready to give up my grandiose wishes to be ideal.

Humility:
Giving Up Who You Wish You Were and Embracing Who You Really Are

In a nutshell, the resolution to our shame is humility—or simply, seeing and accepting ourselves as we really are. But in order to see ourselves as we really are, we must let go of our wishes to be ideal, and as always, letting go of something involves mourning.

By way of review, remember that our shameful feelings and critical self-statements clamor to hold on to our ideal selves and blot out our real selves. This is what the pastor and the pianist in chapter 9 were experiencing in their shameful feelings about their performances. They did not realize that wishes to be ideal lay behind their painful self-criticism.

To resolve our shame, we have to reverse this process. We have to stop shameful feelings and self-recrimination by mourning and letting go of our unrealistic wishes to be ideal. Like the apostle Peter and King David, we must give up wishing and pretending we are better than we are. As we accept the reality of our sins, shortcomings, and limitations along with our strengths and virtues, we embrace who we really are. We become humble and free of shame.

A Model for Resolving Shame

The process of mourning the loss of our ideal selves could be represented as follows:

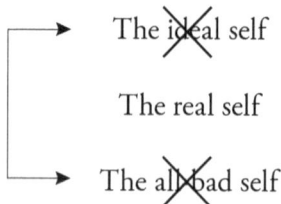

(See chapter 9 for a review of these terms.) The all-bad self and the ideal self walk hand in hand. As we mourn the loss of our wishes to be ideal, we get rid of the all-bad self. Our wishes to be ideal actually hide behind a pious-seeming, all-bad self. The all-bad self tries to whip us into perfection by making relentless statements about how poorly we are doing. These negative self-statements and the feelings they trigger constitute the shame experience.

When we feel the shame of these negative self-statements, we naturally try to get rid of the shame by behaving more ideally. But we need to reverse this process. We need to take the shaming statements as warning signals—warning signals that secretly we have become arrogant and are striving after ideal selves. Framed this way, shame loses its sting and simply becomes a call to let go of an idealized view of ourselves and to become increasingly honest about who we really are.

Mourning the Loss of an Ideal Self

I discovered while talking with a woman on a cruise to Mexico that the story of King David has universal application. She told me she was in the middle of a divorce. Her husband was leaving her for another woman, and we joined in hating the other woman for a moment. It was easy and natural for us to frame the *other woman* as atrocious while bolstering our own sense of being superior human beings. But after a while I got to thinking and began telling her about King David's affair—how he was like the other woman and even worse, how we are all like that other woman if we're honest with ourselves.

She listened intently and said, "If that's true, there's no hope for any of us." She was right on target. Our situation *is* hopeless—utterly hopeless. None of us will ever be the deserving, righteous person we wish to be.

I need to qualify this hopelessness. Its purpose is to lead eventually to a realistic hope. But before the realistic hope can come, we must experience hopelessness for a time as we give up the false hope.

Giving up our false hope for an ideal self is difficult. We have been passionately invested for a long time in our wishes to be ideal. They have inspired and energized us. When we let go of wishes that are so consuming, we experience a temporary despair. But the ideal self on which we have been pinning so much hope is not real. So we must experience this hopelessness if we are to have realistic wishes and hopes about who we are and what we can achieve.

One author describes this hopelessness as the "gift of tears."[1] It is a bottoming-out time as we confront our stark sinfulness and the unbridgeable gap between the sinful self that is and the ideal self that we wish we were. It is a gift to be able to see our real condition and feel desperately sad about it because paradoxically, a hope is born as we face the hopelessness of our condition.

This seems to be the idea behind James 4:9, 10, which says, "Be miserable and mourn and weep; let your laughter be turned into mourning, and your joy to gloom. Humble yourselves in the presence of the Lord, and He will exalt you." Only as we mourn the loss of our false hopes in ourselves, can we experience the exaltation of being known, loved, and accepted by a perfect God.

The apostle Peter and King David experienced this gift of tears. When the cock crowed and Peter realized he had denied Christ, he "wept bitterly" (Mt 26:75). It was an awful moment for Peter. It was also his gift of tears. In that moment he realized he was not the steadfast and loving man he had wished to be. But in that same moment, Peter, disillusioned and hurting, gained a much deeper (and very freeing) awareness of his humanity and of God's deity.

King David's gift of tears started with Nathan's shocking confrontation, "You are the man!" Nathan went on to tell him that the son born of Bathsheba would die. Perhaps it took this much to bring David to his gift of tears. David went from despising God and his Word by doing evil in his sight (see 2 Sm 12:9, 10) to fasting and lying before the Lord all night, asking for the life of his son.

Long before, standing before a giant with only a slingshot in his hand, David knew he was utterly dependent on God. Somehow, in his rise to power, he had forgotten this truth. Now he remembered.

Freeing up Passions for Reinvestment in a Real Self

As with other unrealistic wishes, the point of mourning and letting go of unrealistic wishes to be ideal is to free up our passions for reinvestment in realistic wishes. Mourning the loss of our wishes to be ideal yields two highly desirable outcomes.

First, as we give up our striving to be ideal, we can finally accept love from God and from other people. Until we give up striving, we are so bent on *earning* love through being ideal we cannot take in real love. Real love, first and foremost, seeks and wills the good or well-being of the loved one[2]. Real love also sees through our flaws and faults to our personhood and potential and thoroughly enjoys, cherishes, and roots for who we really are. That's how God loves us and that's how effective parents love their infants and growing children. Both God and effective parents are aware of our faults and helping us outgrow them while generously, joyfully loving us as people.

But in our striving to be ideal in order to earn love, we misunderstand the nature of love. If we are loved only because we appear to be ideal, then we are not really loved at all, because those loving us are only loving the idealized image we present and not the person we actually are. We may be experiencing approval or admiration, but we are not experiencing love. What we are experiencing may be the only connection to others we have ever known, and it may seem necessary to our survival. *But this connection is not love.*

Hinting at the true nature of love, a pastor once said, "I'm not okay; you're not okay, but that's okay." It is only as we give up our wishes to be ideal and settle into the fact that we are not okay that we get a glimpse of what love really is. Love is what God did in Christ. "But God demonstrates His own love toward us, in that while we were yet sinners, Christ died for us" (Rom 5:8). God's love for us is grace-based. It's based on gift, not merits; and it's based on God's will and character. Until we realize that God's love for us reaches out to us precisely while we are messy and on the wrong path (again, like a parent with an infant...or like an adoring human with a precious, sloppy puppy), we are doomed to our contortions, denials, and pretenses that we are something other than the flawed human beings we are.

In *Return from Tomorrow*, George Ritchie illustrates the true nature of love. He relates a time when he had a near-death experience and believes he encountered the person of Christ. As the details of his life flashed before him, George struggled with the self-centeredness and lack of accomplishment that he perceived had been at the core of his life. He wanted to defend himself to the Presence, but...he writes,

> The brightness seemed to vibrate and shimmer with a kind of holy laughter—not at me and my silliness, not a mocking laughter, but a mirth that seemed to say that in spite of all error and tragedy, joy was more lasting still.
>
> And in the ecstasy of the laughter, I realized that it was *I* who was judging the events around us so harshly. It was I who saw them as trivial, self-centered, unimportant. No such condemnation came from the Glory shining round me. He was not blaming or reproaching. He was simply...loving me.[3]

Simply...loving us. We are loved not because we are loveable or have done anything that would earn his love but because love is what God does and who he is. Further, *loving us* means that he knows us intimately and deeply (see Ps 139). He's always thinking about us (see Ps 139:17, 18), and when he thinks of us it is with delight (see Ps 18:19), well-wishing (see Ps 35:27b), and desire to engage with us (see Zep 3:17). He prays for us (see Rom 8: 26, 27, 34) and actively plans for and promotes our well-being (see Jer 29:11). And while it's true that his love for us is based on his grace (free gift) and mercy (will to ease suffering) and in spite of our wrongdoing, it's also a personal love. It's *us* that he actually loves.

As we give up our wishes to be ideal and are finally able to take in real love, there is an added benefit. Once we are loved in this way—wholeheartedly and in spite of our flaws, limitations, and weaknesses—we are better equipped to love others in this way. And this is the only way we'll ever love—because if we are to love one another, we will be loving stumbling and flawed (though often delightful) human beings.

It is indeed humbling and also scary to give up the last vestiges of our efforts to be ideal, to give up pop psychology's banner *you deserve to be loved* and to realize we deserve nothing. It is extraordinary to know we *are* loved and that the love we experience is based on something totally out of our control—the will of the Lover.

Some people will continue to pursue their ideal selves. There is a kind of security in thinking we can merit and thus control love. But others will pass through the gift of tears and will see a vision of their real selves who are unworthy of being loved. They will stop fighting with their unworthiness, and for the first time ever, they will be free simply to be loved. Facing who they are before God, they will be free to accept his grace and love.

King David made this transition. His words after the confrontation by Nathan were as follows: "Be gracious to me, O God, according to Thy lovingkindness; According to the greatness of Thy compassion blot out my transgressions" (Ps 51:1). Suddenly, he knew that love and compassion were all about God and were in spite of his wrongdoing. He was utterly sinful. He had been conceived in and born into sin, and he had acted it out all his life.

David came to know truth and to glimpse the hidden parts of himself. He saw the stark sinfulness that had cowered behind his presumptions of being the *ideal* man of God. And as David confronted the sinful depths of his real self, he was able to trust that God would make him "hear joy and gladness" (v. 8) and give him a new heart, simply because he loved David.

The second outcome of mourning the loss of our wish to be ideal is we then become free to pursue our ideals. Giving up the ideal self does not mean that we give up our ideals. On the contrary, only a real self can do real deeds, and only *real* deeds can fulfill our ideals. Deeds carried out only in our imaginations—and even deeds actually done but done only to promote our own ideal selves—don't amount to much in the final analysis. Further, as we face our failure to live up to our ideals, we may see that there are things that we simply cannot do; and from this place of helplessness, we are especially motivated to lean into God's strength to accomplish through us what we cannot accomplish on our own.

We see this progression in Peter's life. Peter protested to Christ that even if he had to die, he would not deny Christ. But when the time came, Peter could not deliver on his promise until he saw the awful reality of who he was before God. After he had wept over his flawed inability to love Christ the way he truly wanted to—then and only then—was he able to lean into God's strength to love Christ in the ways he wished.

According to church history, when later facing crucifixion, Peter chose to be crucified upside down because he did not want to presume to die as had his Lord and Savior, Jesus Christ. Peter carried out his wish, but only after he had come face-to-face with his imperfection and his inability to do what he wanted to do.

We take hope from stories like Peter's because we see those who are not heroic do noble things. Deep in our souls, we resonate with the unheroic, and when we see ordinary people do the extraordinary, it inspires us. We begin to think that maybe we can do noble deeds too.

There is no conjured, contorted, or contrived idealism in assessing ourselves—only an honest realization accompanied with a real despair that I am, after all, utterly flawed and sinful. Period. No justification, no defense, no extenuating circumstances. Our condition is hopeless, and therein lies the secret—the secret that only the unheroic can do heroic things. Those who strive to fulfill high-flown wishes about themselves cannot do heroic things. But once we know how unheroic we are—once that is no longer an issue for us—we are free to pursue our ideals and to become heroes.

CHAPTER 13

RESOLVING BITTERNESS— PART 1: ENTERING THE PATH OF FORGIVENESS

At the end of the book of Ruth, we see a different Naomi than the one at the beginning of the book. Here is a contented Naomi interacting with the people in her hometown. When she first returned to her homeland, she had said to her kinsman and friends, "Do not call me Naomi (pleasant); call me Mara (bitter)" (Ru 1:20). But here is a new picture, one in which the women gather around Naomi to celebrate the birth of her grandson, Ruth's child. They declare, "Blessed is the Lord who has not left you without a redeemer today, and may his name become famous in Israel. May he also be to you a restorer of life and a sustainer of your old age..." (Ru 4:14, 15).

To these exaltations, Naomi makes no disclaimers, no protestations about how the Lord has dealt bitterly with her. Rather she tenderly takes the little boy on her lap and cares for him. It appears that Naomi is no longer bitter. She has confronted two paths—the path she had longed to walk along with her husband and sons—a path that no longer existed—and the new path life now offered her. Somehow Naomi has left the path that could no longer be, and she has actively and creatively embraced her new life, investing her passions in the real world that was hers to enjoy. How did she so markedly overcome her initial bitterness?

The book of Ruth does not detail the process Naomi went through in resolving her bitterness. But there are certain steps typically taken in overcoming bitterness, and I will illustrate these steps through examining a wife's reaction to being divorced.

Divorce is one of the most widespread causes of bitterness. Either party in a divorce may become bitter, but the abandoned spouse is particularly susceptible to bitterness.

Ana was an abandoned spouse who struggled with bitterness. She thought she deeply loved Isaac, but actually her love was about 80 percent need and 20 percent love. Isaac for his part had reveled in the security afforded him by Ana's deep neediness, but he grew tired of it and fell in love with Val, who seemed much feistier and alluringly independent. He filed for divorce. Ana alternated between expressing hurt, pleading for Isaac to return, and being hostile with many demands. Isaac proceeded unswervingly toward divorce. Ana's intense feelings settled into a cold, hard, hateful bitterness. In order to resolve her bitterness, she will have to mourn and let go of deep-seated longings. There are four steps to this process.

Step 1: Acknowledging we are bitter

Simply acknowledging we are bitter is the first step toward resolving bitterness. Naomi was very upfront about her bitterness, and Ana (in our story) will also have to acknowledge her bitterness.

This can be a very difficult step because it may involve letting go of wishes to be ideal. For example, Ana may have strong motives for wanting to appear as an ideal wife—loving, compassionate, forgiving, and *not* bitter. She could believe that Isaac wouldn't dare leave such a virtuous woman or that her virtue gives her the right to make demands of God about her marriage. But Ana will have to give up her wishes to be ideal and acknowledge her bitterness if she is ever to resolve it.

This is what a psalmist named Asaph did. In Psalm 73, he dealt with very real negative feelings such as envy and bitterness. Describing himself as being in the throes of these negative feelings, he stated that his heart had been "embittered" and he had been "senseless and ignorant…like a beast" before God (Ps 73:21, 22). It is in the context of confessing his bitterness that he made a triumphant statement from which we can all draw security. "Nevertheless I am continually with Thee; Thou hast taken hold of my right hand. With Thy council Thou wilt guide me, and afterward receive me to glory" (Ps 73:23, 24).

Asaph's bitterness did not block his relationship with God. Rather, as he openly confessed his bitterness, Asaph was able to work through it to get to a place of passionate longing for God. "Whom have I in heaven *but Thee?* And besides Thee, I desire nothing on earth" (Ps. 73:25). This psalm demonstrates that becoming passionately spiritual people who walk closely with God does not involve never becoming bitter. Rather, it involves being honest and open about bitterness as we experience it. Like the psalmist and Naomi, we must acknowledge our bitterness in order to resolve it.

Step 2: Taking responsibility for our own bitterness

It is a common myth of bitterness that our bitterness is someone else's responsibility—that we need someone else to change in order for our bitterness to be resolved. Let's say that Ana, like Naomi and Asaph, freely acknowledged her bitterness. In fact, Ana told anybody who would listen about her bitterness! But she told people in a way that blamed Isaac and made him responsible. She regularly engaged in what I will call *bitterness attacks*. These bitterness attacks involved framing Isaac as the bad guy. Sometimes she carried out these attacks in her own mind and sometimes in conversation with other people— some of whom, unhelpfully, would side with her against Isaac.

Indignantly and obsessively, she rehearsed his wrongdoings toward her—his lies, broken commitments, and heartless abandonment. Because Isaac was the abandoning party and because even God hates divorce, it was easy enough to make him look like the culprit.

By blaming and framing him, Ana could make an almost unassailable case that Isaac should resolve her bitterness by coming back to her. This was the point of her frequent bitterness attacks. Ana was not engaging in these bitterness attacks because she was a mean, malicious, or vindictive person but because she longed deeply for Isaac and was unable to imagine life without him. The attacks were a desperate attempt to hang on to her fervent wishes that he would come back.

In order for Ana to resolve her own bitterness, she will have to change her deeply ingrained belief that Isaac has responsibility for—and thus power over—her welfare. She will have to realize she is 100 percent responsible for her own well-being—that she alone is in control of her bitterness and her well-being. Our capacity for well-being is ultimately independent of another's choices.

This change will involve mourning and letting go of two types of wishes basic to bitterness.

The first type of wish is *entitlement wishing* (see chapter 8). Ana's belief that Isaac is responsible for her well-being is actually an entitlement wish. Her entitlement wishes had their origin in infancy at a time when she really *was* entitled to having another human being resolve her misery and make her feel better.

Babies need their diapers changed. They get hungry, tired, and cold. When babies need things, they cry, and something wonderful happens. Mothers and fathers appear. They do whatever needs doing, and the babies feel magically better. As we grow up, we graduate from diapers and bottles. Gradually, we internalize the magic. We learn how to make *ourselves* feel better. But sometimes as adults, we still long for that magic—for someone to step in and make us feel all better.

This was the case with Ana. She longed for another human being to have the power to magically ensure her well-being. She brought these longings to Isaac in marriage. Isaac, however, did not have power over Ana's well-being. Even when they were married, she was not consistently contented. Ana kept believing that if only he would change and love her more ideally, *then* she would be satisfied. Ana had been living in an elusive fantasy world for a long time.

Only Ana can create and take charge of her own well-being. There is no external well-being button another human being can push. Isaac's choice to divorce may be a wrong choice, but he is not and cannot be responsible for Ana's bitterness or for her well-being. To resolve her bitterness, Ana will have to mourn and let go of these entitlement wishes.

Ana must also face and mourn a second set of wishes—unrealistic wishes she has about who Isaac is. Ana wishes Isaac would be faithful to his marriage vows and would love her passionately and exclusively for a lifetime. There was nothing wrong with these wishes, except they were directed toward Isaac. His bond with Ana was quite shallow and fickle. He would feel that way toward any woman because he did not have a great capacity for intimacy.

Isaac always had been terribly idealistic. When flaws appeared in a woman, his feelings for her died. He then would go in search of another woman who seemed flawless, someone he could idealize and feel excited about. This description of Isaac may make it sound like he was at fault. But the point is not to justify or condemn Isaac. The point is to describe what Isaac's pattern of behavior had been for a long time. This is the man Ana chose to marry.

In her own wishful thinking, however, Ana had not bothered to get to know the real Isaac before she married him. She was in love with a false image of him (what she wished him to be) rather than with the real Isaac. She fervently wanted him to be someone he was not.

Bitterness is created by our relentless pursuit of unrealistic wishes toward another person—wishes that are not in line with the reality of who the other person actually is or how he or she habitually behaves. In Ana's dilemma the problem is *not* Isaac's failure to fulfill her wishes; it is the unrealistic nature of her wishes. She just wants Isaac to *love* her and to remain faithful to her—a perfectly legitimate wish. But Isaac is many years away from having the ability to love and be faithful.

Ana *can* change her wishes. She *cannot* change Isaac. She can make her requests and wishes known to Isaac. She can try to creatively negotiate them with Isaac. But should he choose to not grant them—no matter how right and reasonable the requests are and no matter how entitled Ana feels to having these requests granted—she has only two choices. She can either keep wishing and being disappointed, resulting in bitterness, or she can bring her wishes toward Isaac in line with reality through mourning.

Mourning and letting go of both entitlement wishes and unrealistic wishes about other people lead us to a reframing of our premises about them—and about ourselves. It is this reframing that will reverse the whole process of bitterness. But this reframing happens only gradually. At first, the bitterness attacks—the framing and blaming of other people—continue loudly in our minds. Then we may hear a faint voice piping up and saying, "But wait. You can't stay frozen, waiting for others to make everything right. You've got to move forward on your own." Then another wave of blaming and accusing will come crashing down, and once again, we will believe that others *have* to make it all better.

At first, we will only hear this still, small voice of reality between the crashes of bitterness. But we must hang onto that voice, for this is exactly how the resolution to bitterness starts—a faint voice whispering truth. As we hang onto truth, it gets louder.

Step 3: Containing the anger and rage

As soon as we take responsibility for our own bitterness, we are free to work through it and resolve it. As long as Ana is wishing and waiting for Isaac to change in order to resolve her bitterness, she is quite helpless. She cannot work through it.

As she accepts her responsibility to resolve her own bitterness, her next step is to learn how to *contain* her anger—how to simply sit with the anger. As she sits with her anger, Ana lets herself *feel angry*. She tolerates a churning, seething, steaming, stewing, fretting, and fuming feeling inside. Adrenaline is prompting her to *do something*, but there is nothing dramatic to be done. There is no shortcut. There is only a slow, arduous process of working through broken hopes and dreams as Ana learns to manage frequent internal eruptions of anger. (This process provides a whole new understanding of the word *patience*.)

To further clarify what it means to *contain* our anger, consider the two main alternatives to containment—blaming or repressing our anger.

When we blame, we see our anger as someone else's responsibility. Let's reverse the roles in this marriage for a moment and see Isaac in an instance of blaming. While they were still married, Isaac and Ana would often show up late for parties because Ana took too long getting ready. Isaac would become furious and would not simply confront the problem of Ana's lateness, but in a tirade he would tell her she had ruined his whole evening. It wasn't Ana's fault his whole evening was ruined. It was his attitude that had ruined his evening, and that was Isaac's problem. But Ana would accept the blame. She would become overly apologetic and assure Isaac it would never happen again. Ana volunteered to take responsibility for Isaac's anger in order to placate it, and Isaac let her because it provided him with instant relief.

Although Ana, in collusion with Isaac, can pretend the anger is her fault, she cannot resolve Isaac's anger for him. So by blaming Ana, Isaac blocks his own ability to work through his anger, and his unresolved anger settles deep into his soul as bitterness.

The second alternative to containing anger is repression or pretending we are not angry when we are. Consider ways that Ana might try to pretend she is not angry in the divorce process. She could make euphemistic statements by saying, "Everything's fine. God will work it out," or, "I didn't love Isaac anyway. Good riddance," or, "I just love him so much. I want whatever makes him happy." Or she could jump into another relationship in order to pretend that everything is fine and that she has nothing about which to be angry. By any of these means, she might block her *awareness* of her anger, but she would not resolve it. It would stay frozen inside, and it, too, would settle into *her* soul as bitterness.

There is a myth about the resolution of anger. It is the belief that expressing our anger to another person is the key to resolving it. Sometimes expressing our anger to another person is important, but much of our anger resolution involves learning to sit with it and work through it honestly in our own hearts. We may need an objective outsider to help our perspective and to keep us honest. But the main work of resolving the anger behind our bitterness lies in confronting our own unrealistic wishes and assumptions. Even when we do need to express anger to someone who has wronged us, we often need to contain it and work through it to a certain degree *before* we are able to sanely confront anyone else.

The point of containing our anger is not to sit with it forever but to be able to acknowledge and explore our anger so that we can work it through. Even though we seek to work through our anger, we all have times when we slip up. We bitterly blame the person who has disappointed us. During these eruptions, once again, we vehemently accuse and frame the other person as the cause of our misery, wishing desperately that he or she would change and make it all better. (Our wishes die hard.) These eruptions do not mean all is lost, for part of the working-through process is in catching ourselves sooner and sooner and taking responsibility for these eruptions.

We take responsibility for these eruptions by simply apologizing and asking for forgiveness from the person hurt by our eruption. At first, these eruptions will happen frequently. After a while, we will catch ourselves in time to contain the anger within our own hearts without verbalizing it. Jesus knew about our slowness to change and the many slipups that would occur along the path of change when he told us to forgive one another seventy times seven (see Mt 18:22).

Even though Isaac may look like the wrongdoer, Ana also may be doing wrong in framing him as unjustly responsible for her life and well-being, and she may owe him an apology. It is essential in the resolution of bitterness to take responsibility for our wrongdoing. It is only as we do so that we are set free to engage in the rest of the steps for working through our bitterness.

But a word of caution is in order. Taking responsibility for our wrongdoing is really difficult. Learning to face and sit with ugly feelings and impulses like bitterness, anger, and entitlement can be quite draining and discouraging. It may even trigger despair. Therapists can help you be gracious and understanding with yourself as you face these faults and shortcomings, and they can also introduce insight and perspective that can help dislodge these gripping feelings.

So too, they can coach you in techniques such as mindfulness, strategic breathing, and gently shifting awareness to positive images that can help modulate the agitation and turmoil we often feel when facing and resolving anger, bitterness, and entitlement.

But these struggles are not just psychological. They are also spiritual. Remember—or consider—the claims of Christianity to equip you for this spiritual struggle. Christianity teaches that we are forgiven our sins (which bitterness, rage, and entitlement as well as intense wishes for wrong things typically lead to) through believing in Jesus Christ (see Jn 3:16–18; 1:1–14, 29; Acts 4:8–12); that we are deeply loved by God through faith in Christ even as we struggle with ugly faults (see Rom 5:8–10; 8:31–39; Eph 2:4–10); and that again through faith in Christ, we are given the gift of the Holy Spirit to actually empower us to overcome our wrongdoing (see Lk 11:9–13; Jn 14:12–18, 26, 27; Rom 7:24–8:11) and to live fully and joyfully (see Gal 5:22; Rom 14:17).

The Holy Spirit is not just a nice spiritual idea but a real being (like God the Father and God the Son) who loves us humans and is willing to instill us with God's power to become radically better people. He is not, however, a magic pill, and the process of learning to lean into him with our wrongdoings so that he can transform them can be quite daunting. A wise spiritual director can be pivotal as we embark on this journey. Christian spiritual directors invite us to face our sin and weakness while also gently refocusing us from the sin and weakness to God's mercy and graciousness. They help us realize that however awful our badness is, it can simply become a foil for reflecting God's inestimable kindness and grace in unconditionally loving us through faith in Christ. Realizing that we are loved and that God empowers us to change through the gift of his Spirit then becomes the foundation for a deep and tenacious growth far beyond what we can do on our own.

Whether we get help psychologically and/or spiritually to persevere in this difficult process, the final resolution to bitterness unfolds in the following step(s) culminating in forgiveness.

Step 4: Resolving the good-bad split

A good-bad split occurs in bitterness. When we create good-bad splits, we view people unrealistically, framing some as all bad and idealizing some as all good. Although Ana would never put it into these words, she believes Isaac is all bad. He is to blame for her misery. He has no right to hurt her like this. He has committed terrible, unthinkable, and unfair acts toward her. She also believes implicitly that she is all good. Again, she would never say this. It would sound too glaringly proud. But the implicit belief in her bitterness is that Isaac is the all-bad victimizer, and by virtue of having been victimized, she is the deserving (all-good) victim.

Ana will resolve this split as she works to change her attitude in the following ways:

First, she will have to make herself remember *good* things about Isaac. In her bitter framing of Isaac as the one to blame for her misery, Ana may be very resistant to this step. She may protest that he was never any good. It was all deceit. Or she may claim she has no problem seeing goodness in Isaac and may angrily reel off several good characteristics about him, such as the fact that he's good-looking, financially stable, physically fit, and a decent father.

Both lines of response—whether protesting his total lack of goodness or quickly asserting that she already acknowledges his goodness—are actually defenses against recalling Isaac's goodness. If she were to fully remember Isaac's goodness, she would have to think *and* feel about positive memories regarding Isaac—memories involving laughing and playing together, touching times around the births of their children, times when he really heard her as few others had, or times when he went the extra mile for her. These memories would leave her feeling warmly toward Isaac. (Note that this process flies in the face of bitterness. Bitterness would frame Isaac as all bad and would replace warm feelings toward him with hard, cold feelings.) If bitterness frames the other person as all bad, then as we make ourselves recall good thoughts and feelings about the other person, we begin to neutralize the bitterness.

Second, Ana will have to reckon with her own badness. She will need to face and confront the fact that she has done wrong in ways that are really quite similar to those for which she berates Isaac. When she is feeling incensed with Isaac for his lying and betrayal, she will need to realize that she, too, has deceived people or has at times promised other people more than she could deliver. If she is furious at Isaac for having unfairly abused her, whether emotionally or physically, she will have to reckon with the fact that she has also hurt others. Maybe her hurtful behaviors have been much subtler than Isaac's. Maybe she rarely says anything mean to anybody. In fact, maybe she has worked very hard to appear to be Madame Nice. But hurtful behavior is acted out in many ways, and if she honestly looks at her own actions and motives, she will realize she has deeply hurt others at times.

Making herself remember Isaac's goodness as well as her own badness does away with the good-bad split and places Ana on equal footing with Isaac. Just like Isaac, she is a complex mixture of good and bad attributes. As Ana gives up the good-bad split, she further gives up two wishes already alluded to—the wish for a self that could be considered ideal by being so superior to Isaac's alleged badness and her entitlement wishes stemming from her belief that she is the all-good victim and therefore deserves to have Isaac return.

Entering the Path of Forgiveness

Toward the end of the Lord's Prayer, there is a perpetual reminder that we all stand together as sinners. "And forgive us our debts, as we also have forgiven our debtors" (Mt 6:12). In this sentence Jesus exposes the split between the good victim and the bad victimizer once and for all as the prideful illusion it is. The basis of my own forgiveness toward others is in part my own wrongdoing. I can never get away from my own sinfulness, and if I honestly dwell on my own misdeeds, it may instruct me that the offender's actions were not so outrageous or inconceivable after all. We all do very wrong things at times.

As long as Ana chooses bitterness, she does not acknowledge her fundamental equality with Isaac. She remains outraged at Isaac for his wrongdoing and continues to see him only through the grid of her disappointed wishes, and she judges him harshly in light of these disappointed wishes. His personhood is defined as bad in light of the wishes that he has disappointed. Unwittingly, she has seen him only as an object to fulfill her wishes. But this limits and diminishes Isaac's wholeness and personhood. She is not allowing him to be a person in his own right.

Forgiveness restores other people to their rightful wholeness. Ana struggles to acknowledge Isaac's wholeness and thus to forgive him. As she makes herself recall the good and bad in Isaac, she gives up her own wishes toward him and sees him as much bigger than merely an object to fulfill her wishes. She tries to understand his current hurtful behavior in light of hurts from his own past, and she sees him as a struggling human being with needs and wishes of his own—who, like Ana, sometimes hurts others as he grasps to fulfill these wishes and needs.

Forgiveness then involves giving up our good-bad splitting and seeing other people as whole. The process involves letting go of cherished wishes. It's funny. We can *forgive* all manner of sins. We can appear quite generous and magnanimous about the abstract sin that's out there in the world, but considering the sin that disappoints our life's wish, *that* sin we cannot forgive until we let go of the wish.

As we give up these wishes and pretenses, we are on the way to ending bitterness and embracing forgiveness. But the work is not yet complete.

CHAPTER 14

RESOLVING BITTERNESS— PART 2: GIVING UP THE WISHED-FOR PARENT

As we begin to take responsibility for and deal constructively with our bitterness, it eventually becomes necessary to separate anger originating in the past from anger originating in the present. It has been said that 80 percent of our rage actually stems from past interactions, and only 20 percent relates to something happening right now. The overreactions that occur in our bitter outbursts suggest unresolved anger from our past is being triggered by a present interaction. Given what may have occurred in the past, these outbursts may not be overreactions at all. But if we are ever to resolve our bitterness and respond sanely in the present, we will have to deal with past anger.

Ana, for example, had deep-seated anger over early abandonment by her parents. Inadvertently, she placed responsibility on Isaac to remain loyal to her in ways that could somehow cure or make up for those early losses. Her unrealistic wishes toward Isaac placed unfair pressure on him and actually contributed to the very divorce Ana did not want.

Even apart from a painful childhood, divorce is a terrible and excruciatingly painful event. No wonder God hates it (see Mal 2:16). But Ana almost took her own life in the face of Isaac's leaving. This was a tragic overreaction—a reaction triggered by Isaac's leaving but actually based on Ana's childhood experiences of abandonment. The divorce triggered vivid memories and deep despair from a time when Ana's parents were not available to her and there was nothing she could do about it. While Ana really was dependent on her parents for survival, she is not dependent on Isaac for survival *or* for well-being now. Ana, however, certainly *feels* dependent on Isaac for her well-being. She is reliving the anguish of those early years, and Isaac seems to be the cause of it.

In order to get over the feelings of life-and-death dependence on Isaac—and the wishes and bitterness that go along with these dependency feelings—Ana will have to mourn and work through the early losses that are coloring her current experience. Understanding that the marked dependency she's feeling really stems from childhood losses that *can be* worked through—and not from the loss of Isaac which *cannot* be prevented—can bring Ana initial hope; and she will need a wise, skilled therapist to hold her emotionally through the painful work of resolving these devastating losses.

Bitterness may surface in dramatic losses like Ana's as well as in little everyday losses. Consider Meg's problem. In a free-floating conversation, it's sometimes hard to gauge when to enter the conversation. Sometimes we err and interrupt. Sometimes we get interrupted, and we take it in stride. Meg, however, couldn't tolerate being interrupted. When someone accidentally cut off her speech, she would become enraged. In the best-case scenario, she would manage to keep her anger to herself, but stuffing it down inside would cause her to become cold and withdrawn and to exit at the earliest polite opportunity. In the worst-case scenario, she would explode and tell the interrupter that she had not finished and to wait his or her turn. This certainly put a damper on casual conversation!

Meg overreacts. She appears to have a chip on her shoulder—a common mark of bitterness. It is because she is expressing unresolved anger from her past. Meg's father always demanded center stage, and in the day-in, day-out family interactions of her childhood, she was repeatedly cut off by his demands for preeminence.

As a little girl, Meg didn't understand what was happening. She simply adored Daddy and did whatever it took to please him. Meg cooperated fully with her father, who, not altogether aware of what he was doing, ignored and overlooked her as he sought to build his own self-esteem. So Meg experienced abandonment. She was disappointed in a major way in her very healthy wishes to be special. If Meg could trace her bitterness back to its beginnings and could work through the disappointed wishes of the little girl, she would be free to ask the interrupter to let her finish her thought. She could make this request in a mild, easygoing way rather than in an explosion. She might even be able to sometimes just let her point be lost in the normal give-and-take of adult relating.

Letting Go of the Wished-for Parent behind the Rage

In resolving bitterness, letting go of and mourning the wished-for parent behind the rage is the bottom-line task. At this point we have worked through the anger and are beginning to face the *original sadness*. It is also at this point that a common mistake is often made. We often assume that once the rage is attributed to our mother and/or father, the cure for the rage is to express the pent-up rage to the parents and show them how they must change.

If Meg could gain insight into how her father had continually overlooked and overpowered her in childhood and finally have the nerve to confront him—and if her father could see what he had done and change his whole pattern of relating to her—even then Meg's bitterness would not automatically clear up. Why? Because by the age of twenty-five, Meg had made hundreds of people over into the image of her father.

There was a man at the store who had butted in line and elicited in Meg the old feelings of being overlooked. There was the overbearing teacher under whom she had interned and around whom she always felt so small. There was the man with whom she was in love but with whom she found herself in repeated power struggles. There was a friend who was so shy and unassuming that sometimes Meg felt like she herself had become her father as she overpowered this friend who never stood up for herself.

Meg can't go around confronting all the *fathers* she has accumulated over the years. Rather she must deal in her own inner world with the powerful father who is still overpowering a very little girl. Without realizing it, Meg has been carrying this dynamic father-child pair around inside her since childhood. It has become such a part of her character that she often unwittingly recreates a relationship between an overpowering father and a little girl in her interactions with others. Meg needs to do the inner work of making peace with her wishes for the father she never had. This will be a work of sadness—letting go of her deep childhood wishes for a certain kind of love from Daddy. When she has completed her work, the adult Meg can begin to distinguish between the real people that she meets and this overpowering internal father. (By the way, what she found out is that in some ways even her real father needed to be sorted out from this childhood image of an overpowering father.)

Making Peace: Mourning and Acceptance

Sometimes it is legitimate to confront parents with past wrongdoing. They may understand what they did wrong and feel deeply sad about it. Such empathy deepens our closeness as adults.

They may also stay entrenched in denial. They have their own harsh realities they wish to avoid. But regardless of the parents' responses to our confrontation, such a confrontation will not cure the bitterness and may even become a subtle form of blaming the parents.

Bitterness is our own personal defense against long-standing disappointment and loss. Bitterness takes an angry, demanding stance and utters the cry "I deserve better than this!" It holds on to our wishes for better parents. It protects us from the deep sadness of the simple reality that our parents lacked some of the love, warmth, or wisdom we needed as children.

Even if parents, when confronted, realize their wrongdoing, accept responsibility, and want to help the adult children, they still cannot go back in time and undo childhood hurts. In a sense, the adult children stand alone in the task of revisiting the deep sadness from childhood and accepting the realities about their parents' shortcomings and how much these hurt and cost them.

We cannot change the past, and so the main task of adulthood is to make peace with the way things were in childhood. Until we begin this task of mourning and acceptance, we haven't grown up. Rather we remain locked in bitterness and entitlement—children demanding better parents so we can move forward. Like the bewitched stone animals in the witch's winter courts of Lewis's *Chronicles of Narnia*,[1] the embittered person feels frozen in time, waiting for a wished-for parent to give that magic hug and recognition that will free him or her to move forward.

Some childhoods are awful, and a person emerging from such a childhood deserves a red badge of courage. He or she will need a lot of understanding and support to be able to go forward. Other childhoods are not so bad, but the truth is that every childhood has its own brand of scathing. As Calvin of *Calvin and Hobbes* fame puts it, "Those who get nostalgic about childhood have obviously never been children."

Well-being then is attained as we give up the "if only it could have been" world, stop demanding payback, and work through our bitterness to the underlying sadness about the way things were.

If there is a payback, it is that after a long, arduous, touch-and-go struggle, we are freed from our childhood bondage to create new paths for ourselves. It doesn't happen all at once, but gradually, a shift does happen. We begin to experience a wholeness and engagement with life that leaves us feeling it was unquestionably worth it all.

Wishes are custom-made. They are tailored to lend meaning to our lives, protect us from hurt, and guide our energy and choices toward joy. Wishes can serve all these functions, provided we are willing to mourn and let go of wishes that are not realistic. If we continue to pursue wishes that are not coming true, the wishes will hurt us more than they help us.

In this section we have looked at a model for mourning the loss of unrealistic wishes. This model applies to all wishes—whether the wishes come out as entitlement wishes, wishes for an ideal self, wishes to do away with threatening aspects of our world through splitting and spoiling, or the many wishes people devise for attempting to create more ideal relationships and environments.

There are countless wishes—and well over seven billion people wishing them. Many of these wishes have highly individualized content according to the hopes, dreams, and disappointments of the individuals wishing them. But there are certain classes of wishes that are so common as to be almost universal. These include the wishes that we bring to God, wishes for stability or security, wishes to be rescued from our dilemmas, wishes we bring to marriage for ideal partners, and wishes that we might be special.

These wishes, too, need to be held lightly with a willingness to mourn and let go of them if they prove unrealistic. In the following section, universal wishes—and the joy that can come as we begin to understand and let go of them—will be examined and illustrated through the lives of human beings struggling to grow.

SECTION 4

UNIVERSAL WISHES WE NEED TO LET GO OF IN ORDER TO KNOW JOY

CHAPTER 15

THE WISHES WE BRING TO GOD

God sometimes disappoints our wishes and dreams. He has actually promised *in writing* to give us the desires of our hearts (see Ps 37:4), to give us beyond all that we ask or think (see Eph 3:20), or to do anything that two or three of us agree on (see Mt 18:19). Sometimes, though, he does not seem to come through on his promises. Sooner or later, God disappoints us. Disappointment in God can hit us especially hard because for many of us, trusting God means bringing all the disappointments and abuses of the past to him, counting on him to fix them or make them up to us. We hope that here at last is a perfect Father and that the church is guaranteed to be a loving family. We bring intense wishes such as these to God—just as we do to people—and these wishes are often initially disappointed as the following individuals discovered.

Don had been the outcast in his family of five siblings. His mother had simply turned her back on him when her favorite oldest son had beaten Don up. Don came running to the God who roundly condemns favoritism (see Jas 2:1–4). How disillusioned he was to confront some of the same unfairness, competitiveness, and favoritism in the church that he had experienced in his family of origin.

* * *

Andre adored his dad. Then his dad left the family for another woman when Andre was seven. Andre kept adoring his father and simply lived for the yearly contacts at Christmas, but eventually his father missed even these rare get-togethers. Andre came running to the God who never leaves or forsakes us (see Heb 13:5) and repeatedly sought mentoring by pastors, respected men of God who held promise of finally being the ideal father. But these trusted fathers exacted a cost. Locked into a little-boy posture, admiring his mentors and looking up to them for direction, Andre was denying his independent thinking and that sense of easy confidence that goes with manhood. Something was missing with even these fathers, and God the Father seemed far away.

* * *

Sally had been so ashamed of the poverty in her family. Vividly, she remembered the Salvation Army visits at Christmastime, the federally funded school lunches, the stained hand-me-down clothes, and the ridicule of her peers. She came running to a God who richly supplies all things for our benefit (see Phil 4:19). After committing her life to Christ, Sally married a good Christian man who did well financially, and they had darling children whom she was determined would never suffer want. Sally was truly content. Then one day a recession hit, and her husband lost his job. The family was on the verge of losing their home, and Sally was on the verge of losing her faith in God as well.

* * *

Sofia and Carlos struggled with childlessness for years. They wanted a child more than anything in the world and had gone through repeated fertility testing to no avail. When Sofia discovered the God of Hannah (see 1 Sm 1:10–20), she came running and hoping. But God did not answer her prayers like Hannah's. She thought she was pregnant at one point, but it turned out to be a false alarm—a seemingly cruel joke by a sadistic god. With her hopes dashed, Sofia felt the only connection she now had with God was her rage.

* * *

It *can* seem cruel when God invites and then disappoints such intense wishes and yearnings in his people. He may seem like a teasing, impotent, or withholding god, and our outcomes with him may seem simply all too familiar. Nonetheless, the problem, as heartrending as all of the previously outlined struggles are, does not lie in God's nature. He has not wronged us, and if we will stay in relationship with him as we struggle to work through the disappointments, the ultimate outcomes can indeed be beyond all that we ask or think.

A Pattern of Disillusionment

When deep wishes and dreams are thwarted, people will often leave God in bitter disappointment or firmly believing that he is a hoax. An endless quest for wish fulfillment is begun. God is traded in for Buddha, who eventually disappoints us and is traded in for New Age spirituality, which eventually disappoints us and is traded in for politics…or hedonism. The list goes on.

This seems to be the process outlined in Matthew 13:20, 21. Jesus describes the person whose relationship with God will not embrace disappointment: "…the man who hears the word, and immediately receives it with joy; yet he has no firm root in himself, but is only temporary, and when affliction or persecution arises because of the word, immediately he falls away."

When we bring undiluted wishes in the form of subtle demands to God or to anybody, we inevitably experience disillusionment. When it appears that at last I will get what I have yearned for all my life, I embrace him (or her or it) with gusto. When what I have been wanting does not come through in the way I had hoped, I cast him aside. This can become a deeply ingrained pattern as my wishes become the top priority of my life and as I search for the one who can make them come true.

A Gracious Shattering of Narcissism

So why doesn't God give us what we want when he promises he will? How do we explain the major disappointments of Don, Andre, Sally, Sofia, Carlos, and countless others who bring aching desires fervently to a God who promises us the desires of our hearts and then seems to withhold good things from us? If he's all-powerful, why doesn't he just nip our disillusionment in the bud?

Of course we don't always know the answer to that haunting question. God's ways defy explaining, and some of the cruel losses we suffer also defy explaining.

But I believe the answer often lies in the fact that the secret and deepest desire of everybody's heart is to love and be loved. Somewhere deep inside all of us—perhaps buried, quelled, and stifled but there nonetheless—is longing for closeness with other human beings. But in order to grow in genuine closeness with other people, we have to give up our narcissism—that is, our self-absorbed quest for wish fulfillment. We must give it up because in our singular quest for wish fulfillment, we blot out other people. Absorbed in our wishes, we do not see or get to know the other person at all. Rather we make the other person into a means for obtaining what we think we want—that specialness, attention, security, sense of belonging, or prestige for which we have always longed. We cannot experience true closeness with other people as long as we are using them as a means to an end—the fulfillment of our wishes. Rather we need to get to know them in their own right. We cannot love and be loved until we learn to value people (and God) over our wishes.

Thus, God does not always give us our wishes because our singular, self-absorbed quest for wish fulfillment blocks us from what is actually our deepest wish—to love and be loved. He knows that our wishes have another deeper meaning and name, and he knows that learning to let go of wishes—and yet to stay in relationship with the disappointing party—is the only way to deepen narcissism into a capacity for mature love so that our deepest wishes can be granted. It is a paradox then that as we are willing to mourn and let go of our wishes, we grow in our capacity to have still deeper yearnings fulfilled.

We need to hang on to God even through the devastation of our wishes. Ultimately, he really is in our corner and voting for our wishes. "He who did not spare His own Son, but delivered Him up for us all, how will He not also with Him freely give us all things?" (see Rom 8:32). Sometimes, though, our wishes have different names than what we think. We label the deep yearnings of our hearts to the best of our ability, and then we really do need the Holy Spirit, who intercedes for us with groanings too deep for words because we are weak and do not know how to pray as we should (see Rom 8:26). Like infants, we can cry and squirm and give off cues, but we have not necessarily learned the names of our wishes accurately.

So by all means, we need to try to discern the yearnings of our hearts, and then based on our understanding of those yearnings, we must bring our wish lists to God. We also need to have the humility to know we do not necessarily know the names of our wishes. And we need the commitment to God to hang in there, even if by a thread, as he takes us through the painful process of refining our wishes so that we can have what we most want: to love and be loved.

CHAPTER 16

THE STORY OF JOB AND GIVING UP OUR WISHES FOR SECURITY

Pascal, a famous Christian thinker from the seventeenth century, described our often thwarted yearnings for security and stability in life this way: "Whenever we think we have a fixed point to which we can cling and make fast, it shifts and leaves us behind...Nothing stands still for us. This is our natural state and yet the state most contrary to our inclinations. We burn with desire to find a firm footing, an ultimate lasting base on which to build a tower rising up to infinity..."[1]

In rather dramatic terms, Pascal captures our very human yearnings for stability and security. Most of us can relate. We want guarantees that we will continue to enjoy tomorrow those good things we enjoy today, and we try to control our external circumstances accordingly. We save for retirement. We persevere in long-term relationships. We attempt to maintain good health and a stable career.

But there is another subtler way by which we try to gain security and stability in our lives. We try to evolve a set formula by which to live. Starting when we are young, we take in an enormous amount of data about the world and people. We struggle to pull all this data into our life formula. A life formula is a set of assumptions—often unconscious—that guide our behavior and our choices.

By the time we reach adulthood, we may be living our lives according to these kinds of formulas:

- If I am good, good things will happen to me.
- I must leave people before they leave me.
- Every man is out for himself.

Simple acts such as praying when we feel threatened, attending a mixer because we value meeting new people, or giving in to an argument because we don't think that making our point is worth what it will cost the relationship may have complex life formulas behind them.

Whatever our specific life formula, its purpose is to allow us to predict what we think will happen in our lives and then to take control of these future happenings. These life formulas, even though they might be inaccurate in many ways, give us a sense of mastery or control over our world. Life formulas may protect us from getting hurt unexpectedly. (There is some research that suggests that pain hurts less when we brace ourselves for it.) They may also protect us from longing and hoping for things that are not likely to happen. This protective function of our life formulas reflects our wishes for security, stability, and predictability. Our efforts to get security and stability in life are by no means bad or unhealthy. As always, the problem comes when we hold on to our wishes for security, stability, and predictability at the expense of accepting reality.

The story of Job is a story of people who had organized their lives around tight life formulas and how they reacted when their life formulas were threatened.

The story went like this: Behind the scenes, Satan had a talk with God. He challenged God about Job's righteousness, saying that anyone to whom God grants wishes stays true to God, but when God disappoints that person too radically, he or she will not be so righteous. This was perhaps Satan's own life formula, and he set out to prove his premise. He obtained God's permission to torment Job. (God had a bigger plan in mind.)

Job's own worldview and formulas about life stemmed from a profound faith in God. Thus, even when confronted by extreme adversity, Job continued to believe that God was good and worthy of commitment. In Satan's first attacks on him, Job's livestock, servants, and children were destroyed. Job's spontaneous response to this outrage was to worship God. He did not consult with a pastor, mentor, or therapist to work out the proper way of responding! Reflexively, he said, "Naked I came from my mother's womb, and naked I shall return there. The Lord gave and the Lord has taken away. Blessed be the name of the Lord" (Jb 1:21).

In his response, Job did not sin or blame God, and he demonstrated an incredible lack of a sense of entitlement. Even after losing his children, his livestock, and his servants, he did not believe God owed him anything. He was entitled to nothing. Rather his reflexive understanding was that God was entitled to his sovereignty and that Job was a creature and God was the reigning creator. Job won round one in the cosmic match with Satan.

Satan next got permission to afflict Job with painful boils. At this point, Job's wife told him to curse God and die. Job again spoke with an unheard-of absence of entitlement. "Shall we indeed accept good from God and not accept adversity?" (Jb 2:10). In other words, *I deserve no more than I am getting. God has a right to his sovereignty.* Job won round two.

But then Job's friends entered the picture. Job's friends also had lived their lives according to a certain life formula that provided a lot of security and predictability. Their life formula was simple.

- Do good, and get rewarded. Your wishes come true.
- Do bad, and get punished. Your wishes don't come true.

They had organized their whole lives around this formula. They were not about to let go of it easily. Instead they distorted existing data to make it fit into the formula. They said, "This man who has always seemed so righteous now seems to be suffering severe punishment. How can it be? Simple. [Way too simple.] Job sinned, and this *was* punishment after all."

So Job's support system—those who were supposed to be there to help him through this difficult time—set out to convict him. At first glance it seems his support system was his undoing. Under their harassment, Job became presumptuous. He finally overstepped his boundaries with God, so that God ended up confronting him, "Who is this that darkens counsel by words without knowledge?" (Jb 38:2).

And Job repented, "I have declared that which I did not understand, things too wonderful for me, which I did not know" (Jb 42:3).

Job made a slipup here. But over the long haul, his life soundly illustrates his willingness to give up his life formulas in order to grow in a deeper knowledge of who God really was. In all his struggling and lack of understanding and in all his loss—which climaxed in abandonment by friends who deeply misunderstood him—Job never let go of God. He held on for dear life with cries such as "Though He slay me, I will hope in Him" (Jb 13:15) and "As for me, I know that my Redeemer lives, and at the last He will take His stand on the earth. Even after my skin is destroyed, yet from my flesh I shall see God" (Jb 19:25, 26).

Even through the shattering of his life formulas—one of the most painful things we can experience—Job held on to his faith in God. Most people let go in search of someone else who can fit into their life formulas and not shatter their whole existence. But Job didn't go looking for someone else to fit his life formula. He held on to his relationship with God. And an amazing thing happened. He came out the other end of his trials and sufferings with a deeper knowledge of God in all his unapproachable awe and with a settled awareness of himself as an ignorant creature before God. This is the great hallelujah chorus to Job. The subsequent restoration and increase of his fortunes is almost inconsequential compared to this great transformation in his awareness. Satan was wrong. There was at least one man who loved God for God, holding on to him through the shattering of many wishes.

The Wish for Security...and Giving It Up When New Data Doesn't Fit Old Formulas

As seen in the case of Job's friends, clinging to outmoded life formulas can freeze us into an inability to perceive new data. One of the hardest things in life is allowing ourselves to acknowledge that the old formulas don't fit like they once did—and saying to ourselves, "Wait a minute. What's going on here? I don't get it. This doesn't fit."

It can be very difficult to acknowledge that we do not understand what is happening. So we contort new information (and new people) to fit into the familiar secure patterns. Again, this is what Job's friends did. They distorted new data to make it fit old formulas. Job was suffering, and therefore, he must have sinned to merit such suffering. So he just needed to repent and be delivered. Then he would prosper again.

We sometimes see people in so-called dysfunctional family systems trying to recreate life experiences according to secure life formulas. For example, the woman who grew up in an alcoholic family repeats her family formula and is now getting her third divorce from an alcoholic husband. Throughout her childhood her world, which was governed by an alcoholic father, had been a chaotic place. Perhaps she had come to define her own role in life as an organizer of that chaos. Marrying alcoholic men then allowed her to retain her set formulas about the world and her role in it.

Or consider the case of the black sheep of the family who keeps his position as a black sheep even through adulthood by compulsively alienating any new people he meets. In this way, he avoids struggling with thwarted longings to be loved and the risk involved in finally opening himself up to love. He is able to maintain a sense of sameness and of predictability in his life.

It might seem that people who have grown up in such painful circumstances would be ready to adopt a new formula by which to live. But our wishes for security and sameness can sometimes make pain seem preferable to facing our fears of the unknown. If what we have experienced of life and love have been tenuous, we may not dare to let go of the tiny foothold we have in order to try something new. So strong is our wish for stability that we may find ourselves recreating painful circumstances in our lives just to hold on to our secure life formulas.

Even scientists struggle with issues of giving up old life formulas. The scientists who first encountered the truths of quantum physics literally went into despair. They hated what they were discovering because it shook and shattered the very foundations of an orderly universe as they knew it. Unlike Job's friends, however, these scientists chose to let go of their overly simplistic moorings and go where truth led them. But first, they had to give up their wish for the old security.

Children also must give up their life formulas. In his exquisite studies of the unfolding of a child's thought life, Piaget[2] observed that children need to go through a time of disequilibrium—of loss of balance—in order to mature. He discovered that children use two processes to organize the things they learn about the world. By a process called *assimilation*, children fit the universe into ways of thinking that already exist within themselves. By a process called *accommodation*, children adapt to the unsettling news that the big, vast, awesome universe does not fit so neatly into their existing structures after all. They give up the neat little categories and structures they once thought explained everything. They grow up.

These are natural, innate human processes—assimilating and accommodating—embracing the many losses of balance and of security in order to embrace a bigger world and a bigger self. Scientists, saints, children, struggling human beings…no matter who we are or what we do, we all need to let go of our secure life formulas and enter into a space of disequilibrium—of not getting it, of chaos—in order to grow.

In a charming children's book titled *If You're Afraid of the Dark, Remember the Night Rainbow*, Cooper Edens confronts hanging onto life formulas that no longer work for us with winsome words of wisdom like those found in the title. Are you afraid of the dark? His fanciful solution: remember the night rainbow. Edens goes on to offer many whimsical solutions to life's dilemmas such as: If you can't find your key, get rid of your house. If your bus is delayed, get aboard a speedy cloud. If things are turning out wrong, use cookie dough to make your own happy ending.[3]

This is not just wishful thinking or a blind pursuit of silly wishes. It is a shaking up of cherished rigidities so that we can be startled into letting go of the old ways to embrace the new when the old ways stop working. This is the main hope and the great moral of Job's story. The astounding step Job took was that he gave up what he thought he knew about God in order to embrace a bigger God.

George MacDonald, a hero of C. S. Lewis and his mentor, lauded this kind of *not knowing* in a prayer. "But Thou shalt at least find faith in the earth, O Lord, if Thou comest to look for it now— the faith of ignorant but hoping children, who know that they do not know, and believe that Thou knowest."[4]

The dogmatic and black-and-white thinkers cling to the security of the known and the well-established. They cannot let themselves know that they do not know. But Job gave up his wish for security— much of what he thought he knew about God and about life—and came away with a far more realistic and mature vision of who he was and who God was.

CHAPTER 17

THE UNFULFILLED WISHES
OF MARRIAGE

It is very common to bring unfulfilled wishes from childhood and plop them squarely in a spouse's court. Behind the thrill of being in love is often the hope that I have found someone who can love me in the ways I have always longed to be loved. At last, I can make my childhood wishes come true.

Being in love is a nice jump start to marriage. But being married—as being in any long-term relationship—is a process of getting to know the uniqueness and surprises of who the other person is. It's also about mourning the loss of idealized expectations (wishes) about that person (expectations you may not even realize you have until they are disappointed).

What follows is a look at a wife first and then at a husband and their struggles to work through unresolved wishes from childhood that are blocking closeness in their marriage.

A Wife's Wishes

Sarah and Jack were in the third year of what was a second marriage for both of them. Sarah resented Jack's not paying enough attention to her children. She wanted Jack to spend more time with her eight- and ten-year-old daughters. Her wishes—which had become demands—were becoming a constant source of friction between them. It was hard for Sarah to let go of her wishes. It seemed so *right* to want her daughters to be treated better.

Little girls' wishes

From the little girls' perspective, they were excited about their new daddy. He was so much more attentive to them than their birth father had been. He giggled at their jokes. They were just sure their baseball game had improved because of his coaching, and he would read them stories as though he were the actual characters, screwing up his face in truly funny ways. His new daughters adored him and courted him. But when he was not available to them—even after their best attempts to charm him into another game or just one more story—their faces fell. They would be terribly disappointed, and they had no finesse in hiding their feelings. (Nor did they want to. Sometimes Daddy seemed to waver a little if they got sad enough.)

A valuable frustration of wishes

This was the part Sarah couldn't bear. She could not stand seeing her daughters look so pitifully sad. In those moments she thought Jack was harsh and unreasonable, and in her anger at him, she had difficulty loving him.

In reality, the girls needed to learn to deal with these disappointments so they would learn how to deal with the natural losses that would occur in other relationships later in life, especially relationships with men. Fathers need to say no to their daughters sometimes. Always gratifying a child's wishes leads to unrealistic expectations in life. A young girl can be the center of her daddy's world, but one day as an adult in a world of seven and a half billion people, she will become less special. Fathers who give too much special attention to their daughters make the transition from home to the world difficult.

While it is all right to sometimes frustrate a child so that he or she comes to understand the real world, there is a balance too. Too much frustration of wishes, as noted in Ephesians 6:4, can be harmful. It can lead to a child giving up in a quest for closeness with others. The child can come to feel undesirable or start to misbehave in attention-seeking ways.

To further complicate this balancing act between gratifying and frustrating a child's wishes, the child's needs change with age. The infant needs to be catered to a lot. The toddler and then the growing child need to be weaned gradually from this catering and to learn that others have needs too. This balance in frustrating versus gratifying wishes is key to the emotional maturation of the developing child. Such a balancing act requires much discernment in parents. Actually, Jack was maintaining a fairly good balance.

A high cost to acting out wishes

Sarah was overreacting. Her response to the interactions between Jack and her daughters was out of tune with what was actually happening. She was acting out of a past rather than current reality. She was acting out unconscious wishes rooted in her *own* history. Acting out wishes is what happens when we translate our past wishes into present day demands. Thereby, we save ourselves from having to discover and to deal with our old unmet wishes in their proper context.

Sarah wished Jack would *always* gratify her children so that she could pretend everything was idyllic in her current family. In this way, she could avoid dealing with her own unmet wishes. But Sarah's attempt to act out her own childhood through her daughters was creating a double bind for the family. On the one hand, if Sarah got her way, it would be harmful for her daughters, but on the other hand, as Jack resisted her wishes, her ongoing demands put a strain on their relationship as well as on Jack's relationship with his stepdaughters.

Jack had grown up under a critical, domineering mother, and he tended to react negatively toward domineering people. He had begun to feel this way toward Sarah. He was even feeling resistant to spending time with his stepdaughters, whom he otherwise enjoyed.

The wishes behind the wishes

Sarah came into therapy seeking help for her daughters, but as we explored the conflicts, she realized perhaps *she* needed help in resolving losses from her own childhood to get a clearer perspective on what was happening with her daughters. So to uncover the childhood wishes behind her unrealistic adult wishes, Sarah and I began to piece together her background.

Sarah had been the pampered center of her mother's world until age three, which was when her baby brother was born. From that time on, Sarah was clearly—and painfully—playing second fiddle. But Sarah was gutsy. She retaliated and set out to win Daddy's heart. She was beguiling and persuasive, and she appeared to have won him over. It felt like a triumph. In the face of her mother's obvious preference for men, little Sarah had won the kingpin.

The great big "So there!" that she nurtured in her heart did not, however, erase the sadness and emptiness she felt in the loss of her mother. She wished for an idyllic relationship with Daddy that would soothe all her hurts, make her feel special rather than demoted, and assure her that she didn't need her mother anyhow. But underneath these wishes, the sadness and emptiness surrounding the loss of her status and closeness with her mother lay undisturbed and unresolved.

Her defensive wishing had been acted out in many ways over the course of Sarah's childhood and into her adulthood. But the underlying dynamic remained unchanged. Sarah intensely craved her father's affection and attention so that she would not have to face her sadness and emptiness regarding the loss of her mother.

As Sarah successfully gained her father's attention, it became a covering for her pain. Because it masked underlying loss, her craving for her father's attention became an addiction. All through her childhood, she would turn to her father again and again for a *fix*. This addiction to male attention was acted out through a guilt-ridden but driven promiscuity in her teen years. Now it was being acted out with Jack and her own daughters.

For Sarah, then, the temporary and harmless dejection on her daughters' faces when they were disappointed by their stepfather was tapping into a far greater pain. It reminded her of those rare occasions in her own childhood when her father had failed to cater to her wish for specialness. As a child, when her father failed to meet her longings for attention, there was suddenly no buffer between her and the pain she experienced about her mother, and she would plummet into dark despair. Now when she saw her daughters confronting their losses, she could not see those losses as natural and necessary. She could only see them as catastrophic like her childhood losses had felt. It was as though Jack's healthy frustration of her daughters took away Sarah's own inner buffer, and she had to confront overwhelming sadness and emptiness from her own past.

A resolution

There were several steps to the resolution of this couple's conflict.

First, Sarah was willing to consider that there might be something wrong with her perspective—that maybe the problem was not all Jack's. This can actually be the most difficult step in resolving marital problems. Blaming one's partner can bring a type of relief. But Sarah took responsibility. Instead of continuing to demand that Jack change *his* behavior, she began to realize that part of what she was wanting was not realistic.

Secondly, Sarah was willing to explore the childhood wishes lying behind her current unrealistic wishes. As she explored her own defensive wishes toward her father, she began to understand how much his over gratification had cost her. From this perspective she could begin to appreciate and respect Jack's saying no to the girls.

Finally, Sarah was willing to do the painful work of facing and working through the losses behind the wishes so that she would no longer need the wishes to defend against the losses. And Jack could support her through this painful process. He was quite willing to listen to and care for his wife once he could get out from under the *bad guy* role.

A Husband's Wishes

Tony's story is the story of a husband's unfulfilled wishes. As a little boy, Tony had to sort through quite a dilemma. He had to somehow create order and safety out of a world in which his mother often cried in terror, a little boy cowered in the corner with his sisters, and Daddy—the big, strong protector of the family—would suddenly turn into a raging monster.

In this dilemma there was one bright spot. Tony's mother really loved him. Granted, she loved him too much. Because she felt abandoned by her husband, she loved Tony as though he were both her little boy *and* her husband. She was too close to him, too needy of him, and as he grew, she had difficulty letting go of him and encouraging him toward independence. But her love was a very genuine cornerstone in Tony's life—something reliable, steady, and incredibly warm around which Tony could orient himself and grow.

The haven that his mother afforded him, however, would crumble under the onslaught of his father's physical abuse of his mother. So at a very young age, when he barely had the words to say these things, Tony began creating a protective fantasy world in his heart. In this fantasy world, it was not hard to imagine his mother as a wonderful, all-good fairy princess. It was an obvious next step to write off his father as an all-bad monster. In a little boy's wisdom, Tony created a good-bad split that helped organize the chaos of his young world.

The truth was that Mother was not really ideal. Nor was Father altogether evil. But in this imagined world of monster and princess, Tony now had a simple formula by which to live his life—avoid Dad and cling to Mom. His fantasy and wishes were buying him security, predictability, and a little slice of seeming heaven—a wonderful mother—in a harsh, unsteady world.

His fantasy and wishes helped Tony negotiate a very difficult childhood, but there were hidden costs to the wishful fantasies. Tony's choice to write off his *monster daddy* was understandable, but the problem was that somewhere in this monster lay the secret to the little boy's own manhood.

As Tony resolved to avoid his father at all costs and to never grow up to be like him, he successfully killed off the monster. But as he killed off the monster, he unwittingly also killed off his own manhood—his ability and right to be aggressive and to cross the bridge from an infant's intense love affair with Mommy to manhood.

And while his positive framing of his mother was a valuable source of warmth and nurture for Tony, his relationship with his mother also had hidden costs. Tony was committed to his mother in a way that made it difficult for him ever to leave her. He vowed he would never hurt her. Although never stated, Tony understood his mother's intense fear of abandonment. He sensed the wishes not to be abandoned that prompted her to endure the beatings and stay with Tony's father. If Tony hurt her by leaving, he would feel as though he were as mean as his father. Besides, why would he want to leave her? With her, he was a knight in shining armor, and this was a status he could get in no other place. When you become a knight in shining armor at the age of two, there's no place to go but down. Anything else feels like a demotion.

The rage

As a man, although Tony felt dominated by his mother, he could not psychologically separate from her because of her seeming fragility… and his own. Even though he left home, launched a stable career in finance, and married, he really never had cut the apron strings. Part of him wanted to be a man, out exploring and mastering new worlds, and part of him wanted to stay securely in his mother's world. It seemed the latter part always won out. In spite of his career accomplishments, Tony had a deep-seated fear he could not make it in a man's world. And in the face of this fear, his mother's attention felt reassuring and necessary.

The upshot was that secretly Tony felt trapped—even seduced—by his mother. Entrapment leads to rage. He was furious at her while at the same time protecting her from his fury because he believed she was too fragile to handle it. In addition, he wanted to keep the comforting myth of the all-good mother alive. It was a vicious cycle.

So Tony carefully detoured his rage elsewhere. He had two main detours—his wife and pornography. He resented and picked at his wife mercilessly. She would try to please him, but somehow she never gave Tony the special treatment a man of his status deserves. Frustrated, she did not realize that an adult peer wife could never live up to an idealized and adoring mother. Tony's wife was a mere mistress. The real wedding had already happened before Tony was three.

Regarding pornography, in Tony's fantasies, he was very hostile, demeaning, and aloof with women who pursued him desperately. This was an obvious expression of rage stemming from his fury at feeling so entrapped by his mother. But sidetracking his rage in this way allowed him to preserve the fairy-tale, all-good mother who made him feel so special.

Moreover, in a twisted way, Tony's deep-seated shame about his dependence on his mother was salved. After all, in his fantasies it was obvious he wasn't the clingy, dependent one! In his fantasies he felt quite independent. But having his passions tied up in pornographic fantasies was not making for full and sane living.

Letting go of the wish for an ideal mother

A failing marriage as well as a pervasive dissatisfaction with life prompted Tony to seek help. As he began to explore his life, Tony could see the way he kept detouring anger from his mother in order to keep his wish for an ideal mother alive. He understood the little boy's need for an idealized mother to ward off the terror of his dad's violent episodes. He also came to understand what his idealized relationship with his mother was costing him. The repeated detouring of his anger at his mother was destroying his marriage and was fueling a destructive compulsion.

As he began honestly looking at these things, he came to realize his mother was not as idyllic as the little boy had imagined her to be. As he began to experience how much her neediness had cost him, he began to feel angry toward her. But he was experiencing his anger in a safe place, therapy. In his therapy he could take responsibility for his anger and work it through constructively rather than acting it out against his mother in destructive ways. Embracing his anger constructively allowed him to mobilize the healthy aggression needed to separate from his mother.

Tony finally began to figure out a way to avoid acting out the destructive rage his father had always exhibited while still having the freedom to mobilize the aggression he needed to end his dependency on his mother. He had to give up his wishes for a secure, predictable, black-and-white world in which Mother was all good and Father was all bad. He had to embrace in a modified form some of his father's aggressiveness, and, in a way, he had to abandon his mother. As he did this, he finally was able to resolve the little boy's terrors and leave home.

CHAPTER 18

TRAGIC CHOICES BEHIND VICTIMIZATION

Francesca has been in an abusive marriage for fifteen years. It began when her husband started pushing her and then escalated into hitting and slapping. Her injuries have required medical attention, and the emotional damage has been devastating. She has been counseled to leave him by many friends, loved ones, and counselors. Those who know her feel her life is in danger, and they have offered support in getting her out of her current living situation. But Francesca has not taken any steps to protect herself. It is as though she *cannot* leave her husband. How has she stayed so long with someone who mistreats her so horribly? And why? It's because of unrealistic wishes. She will never be able to make sustained healthy choices for her life unless she is willing to uncover and mourn the loss of the wishes behind these unwise, harmful choices.

A Tricky Case of Entitlement

Francesca has a wish that is perfectly logical at first glance. She wishes for the abuse to stop, and she wishes to be treated as she deserves. This could be a healthy wish. Obviously, Francesca *does* deserve better treatment. No husband has a right to treat his wife in this egregious manner.

But Francesca takes the wish to be treated as she deserves a step further. She concludes that because what her husband is doing is wrong, the responsibility for change is in his corner. She counts on him changing his behavior because it is the right thing to do and because he owes it to her. This is a highly unrealistic wish. It is very unlikely that her husband will stop abusing her simply because she deserves better treatment.

Hanging on to these entitlement wishes, however, Francesca passively and wistfully waits for her husband to change while enduring steady bouts of abuse. Francesca has already tolerated fifteen years of abuse, and she is likely to tolerate another fifteen years. If she is ever to get out of this desperate situation, she is going to have to give up her wishes and take responsibility for protecting herself. Rather than waiting for her husband to change, she must take critical action to set firm limits to stop his abuse.

When Love Becomes Need

But Francesca feels desperately needy of her husband, making it seem almost impossible to set a serious limit. One obvious limit would be to leave him, but feeling utterly without resources, Francesca is as terrified to leave him as she is to stay with him. Thus, deep feelings of neediness—wishes to be taken care of—block Francesca from taking action. What if she does set a firm limit and says, "I'm going to leave you if you ever hit me again," to her husband? Or what if he is so dangerous that she simply leaves? Imagine the first day after she takes initiative and settles herself in a safe place. She feels very relieved and wonders how she tolerated her husband's outbursts for so long. On the second and third days, she continues to feel very relieved. It feels so freeing not having to be ever vigilant to avoid setting him off. But by the fourth day, she begins to feel a little lonely, and by the seventh day, this awful, aching emptiness sets in—excruciating feelings stemming from a childhood void that she had sworn to herself she would never have to face again—accompanied by taunting words of low self-esteem: *You'll never find anyone better. This is all you deserve.*

At this point, life with her husband is looking better. After all, *anything* feels preferable to this void. What Francesca is now experiencing is a deep *neediness* toward her husband. When we use people to fill voids from our pasts, we are *needing* them rather than *loving* them. This neediness may create very strong feelings toward the other people, but these feelings are very different from love.

When Victimization Becomes a Choice

Consumed by her neediness, Francesca is now open to returning to her husband, and once again, she is vulnerable to believing his empty promises for reform. Perhaps she even assumes responsibility for their difficulties, saying to him with repentance, "It was silly of me to go. I'm so sorry. I know you're going to change. We'll work this out together." But they both know he will abuse her again.

At this point victimization becomes her choice. There are forms of victimization and abuse that are totally the perpetrator's fault—concentration camps, muggings, rape, child abuse, and stalking. But sometimes what we call victimization between adults is actually a two-way contract. It may even be called seduction. It is often a matter of one person making untrue promises, the other person believing them, and both colluding to put their signatures to a contract with unreality. A *victim* of such seduction may protest, "He lied to me! He made promises that he didn't keep." But we are always responsible for discerning reality, and the bottom line in such seduction is that we are not deceived by the other person's persuasiveness but by our own wishes—our own fervent desire to believe what is not true but what would be so wonderful if it were.

Malcolm Muggeridge, a wise journalist and author from the twentieth century, put it like this: "People, after all, believe lies, not because they are plausibly presented, but because they want to believe them. So, their credulity is unshakeable."[1] Or as the author of *Women Who Run with the Wolves*, Pinkola Estes, put it so simply, "The naïve woman agrees to remain 'not knowing.'"[2] Or as Calvin Miller in his rich Christian allegory said, "The hardest lies which we must circumvent are those our troubled, unsure hearts invent."[3]

By just such a process of self-deception, Francesca, tormented by her haunting childhood voids, lapses back into a fantasy world where one day soon her husband will reform and stop abusing her. Thus Francesca *chooses* to go back to her husband because the loneliness of being apart from him is *too* lonely, because she doesn't know where the money to live will come from, and because abuse feels preferable to the risks involved in figuring out how to master life on her own. However dire the circumstances prompting her return to life with an abusive husband, her return is nevertheless a choice. She sees the benefits as outweighing the costs.

I don't want to minimize the fact that this is a tragic choice, selected from no good options. Many of us may never have to face the kind of choice in which there is terror wherever we turn. Nonetheless it *is* a choice. It is pivotal that this woman learn to see her own choice in her victimization. It is only as she sees her ability to choose for herself that she can begin to realize the power to protect herself from this man. As long as she sees herself as a helpless victim being acted upon, she must wait for him to change.

There *is* an upside to the belief that she is a helpless victim. A rescue fantasy goes along with this belief—the wish that because she is helpless, someone will therefore step in and rescue her and make her life all better. In a terrifying and comfortless marriage, this fantasy provides compelling comfort. But it is a fantasy that needs to be mourned.

The Mourning Process

There are several wishes behind Francesca's choice to stay with an abusive husband. There are

- entitlement wishes,
- wishes for another human being to fill her childhood voids rather than her taking responsibility for working through these voids, and
- wishes to be rescued from perceived helplessness or to be taken care of.

Letting go of these wishes will require a mourning process. Francesca will need to put her unrealistic wishes into words. Often the victimized person will protest and say, "But there's no unrealistic wish here. I just want to be treated decently." This is a subtle assertion of entitlement that postpones the responsibility of facing her unrealistic wishes. Francesca struggles to put these wishes into words. Perhaps her wishes reflect romantic longings: "I wanted my husband to be a lover and friend, my best friend—someone I could feel terribly passionate with at times and at other times just be calmly and quietly understood. I wanted to be able to glance across the room and catch him looking at me admiringly and know that I'm a desirable woman." Or her wishes may reflect longings for security and status, "I never dreamed of having money and a home like this before. I grew up poor. He swept me off my feet. It's all so grand. If only he'd stop the abuse, this would be a Cinderella story. I don't want to give it all up. I was a nobody before." Or maybe her wishes are more basic. Maybe she feels that this is as good as it gets and her unstated wish is, "If I don't rock the boat, maybe the damage will be minimum." Whatever her particular wishes are, putting them into words allows her to face and work through the longings that are keeping her in a life-threatening relationship.

The next step will be to confront the wishes and her longings with reality statements—statements that include unstinting descriptions of her husband's abuse; the reality that as things now stand, he will most likely abuse her in the future; and other aspects of the stated wish that have not come true. In these reality statements, she will need to be careful not to frame her husband as totally bad. Realistic statements must include any attractive aspects of her husband that left her longing for him in the first place. Framing him as all bad would simply be an attempt to cut off her longings and would short-circuit the mourning process.

As she confronts her wishes with reality statements, she will sadly and reluctantly come to the awareness that her husband is who he is—a struggling human being who frequently acts out his anger and anguish in ways that are so very wrong and destructive. She will realize she must take charge of her own well-being if she is ever to be safe and at peace.

Changes in the Woman

As Francesca lets go of her wishes or idealized expectations toward her husband, she will experience several shifts in her attitude toward him. First, she will become capable of loving him. In tolerating his abuse, Francesca had always felt like she was exhibiting the height of unconditional love. But she was needing her husband, not *loving* him; she did not even really know her husband. Rather she based their relationship upon an idealized or wished-for man who lived only in her imagination. It was this idealized man that Francesca was so deeply drawn to, not her husband. Only as she lets go of her wishes for this ideal man will she be free to see her husband as he really is—a short-tempered, abusive, demanding, demeaning, struggling human being who is surprisingly nice at times, sexually desirable, and reliable in bringing the paycheck home. He is a mix of good and bad with both great potential and stark limitations. Only as she sees and accepts him as he really is will she truly be able to love him.

This is what unconditional love means—that we see others as they really are, figure out a way to understand them rather than condemn them, and accept them in their struggling condition, even though those very struggles hurt us deeply. That's the way God loves us. "But God demonstrates His own love toward us, in that while we were yet sinners, Christ died for us" (Rom 5:8).

As Francesca mourns and lets go of her wishes, a second internal shift will happen. She will be able to forgive her husband. It may seem like she was forgiving him all along, but she was not. She was simply being abused and cleaning up the abuse with the magic washcloth of her wish. She fervently hung on to the unrealistic wish that her husband would change radically.

That is not forgiveness. In fact, her unrealistic wishes made forgiveness impossible. As long as she held her idealized wishes toward her husband, she could see him only in light of her disappointed or devastated wishes. Her feelings centered around the devastation she felt in his ongoing horrific abuse of her. Her repeated devastated wishes inevitably led to bitterness toward him.

Escalating bitterness comes as a result of repeated disappointment or devastation and is the opposite of forgiveness. In forgiveness, we work at seeing the person who has disappointed or wronged us as being larger than the hurts or wrongs committed. Forgiveness does *not* mean that we ignore, minimize, or permit the hurtful behavior toward us. It does mean that we work to see the offender in light of his total personhood rather than merely judging or defining him in light of the harm done to us.

Without lessening the horror of the abuse, at some point Francesca will need to see her abusive husband in a larger light. In struggling to see his whole personhood, Francesca will need to work at seeing many aspects of her husband. She will need to acknowledge his good and bad qualities (see chapter 13). She will have to take into account his past, present, *and* future. She will have to remember

- a past in which he, too, was wounded;
- the present, in which he is unjustly acting out that wounding; and
- a future in which he has potential for repentance and redemption or for becoming hideously more set in his ways.

She has the opportunity to use her hurt as a lens through which to see his pain. She will then see him as a struggling human being so blinded by his own self-centeredness and so lost in cycles of repetitive damaging behavior that he unwittingly robs himself of the connections with other people that make life rich and worth living.

When Francesca sees her husband as a whole person, she will find her bitterness transforming into forgiveness. She will also be able to mobilize realistic anger and aggression that will enable her to set the boundaries needed to protect herself. The point is that no matter what *he* does, she will never be whole until she mourns and lets go of her unrealistic wishes toward him.

Finally, as Francesca mourns and lets go of her unrealistic wishes toward her husband, she will be able to set *realistic limits* on him. It is ironic that as she loves and forgives him for the first time, she is also free for the first time to set limits on him—quite possibly to leave him as often proves necessary with physically abusive people. But the capacities for loving, forgiving, and setting limits on another person go together because they all depend on a common denominator— giving up our unrealistic wishes toward the other person so that we can see him or her realistically.

Francesca needs to see her husband more realistically in order to set limits on him for three reasons.

First, not until she really sees that he is abusing her will she be able to set limits on the abuse. Until then, she is living according to the way she hopes he will treat her, expecting him to change and never abuse her again. She is not facing how he really *is* treating her. As she faces the reality of his abuse, she will feel angry—even outraged—and will be motivated to take responsibility for setting the limits needed to end the abuse.

Second, in her unrealistic wishes toward him, Francesca is seeing her husband as the source of her well-being. As long as she sees him this way, she cannot set effective limits on him. Her unrealistic wishes toward him make her feel far too needy of him. In this state of mind, she reaches the end of her rope, bluffs him, and gets him to promise to change. But as long as she sees him as the source of her well-being, she cannot reinforce realistic limits on him when he cycles back into abuse. Again, she is too needy of him, and they *both* know there are no teeth to her limits.

Third, as she comes to see her husband more realistically, she will also come to see herself more realistically. This, too, is essential to her capacity for setting limits. As she stops seeing her husband as larger than life, she will stop seeing herself as littler than life—she will take back the power she has unknowingly been giving away to him. When she stops seeing her husband as an idealized source of well-being, she will be able to take increased responsibility for her own well-being. As she takes responsibility for her own well-being rather than depending on someone else as her source, she will no longer believe she needs to accept abuse in exchange for being cared for. She will be able to tolerate the risk of losing the relationship, which may well happen with the setting of effective limits. She will know she does not need her husband in order to survive—physically or emotionally.

Resolution

The solution to problems such as abuse may seem obvious to outsiders looking in. They would tell the abused person to leave... yesterday. But as has been indicated before, the intense wishes behind our seemingly foolish choices can make an obvious choice quite difficult to make. Even if an abused woman comes to understand the unrealistic wishes that have compelled her to stay with the abuser, choosing to take charge of her own life will still be very difficult.

Abuse can be life-threatening. Abusive partners are often brutal and menacing. Real-life fear can interact with deep-seated wishes in influencing victims to stay with their abusers. The situation is complex and dangerous. Sometimes abused women do need for someone to step in and actively encourage and assist them in moving to safety. (Although rescue fantasies are often unhealthy, there *is* a time to try to rescue, and a professional can help discern when rescue is appropriate.) Abused women may not always have the luxury of the time required to mourn and let go of their unrealistic wishes and make healthier choices. They may need to stay alive first and come to grips with their own choices in their victimization later.

But one of the toughest dilemmas faced in domestic violence shelters is the tendency of women to return home to the abuser. Ultimately, if the abused woman is to resolve her abuse, she will have to face her choices and the fervent, unrealistic wishes behind those choices.

Any woman committed to this kind of growth and change will need a great deal of support from wise and caring people who can empathize with the great losses involved while firmly confronting her resistance to change. Our core wishes die very hard, and trading them in for reality can be the hardest bargain we ever strike. But in the case of women who suffer abuse, embracing reality is essential to survival.

CHAPTER 19

WISHES HIDDEN BEHIND BUSINESS CONTRACTS

Wishes are expressed not only in the family and intimate arena. They are also expressed in the work world. In fact, politics in the workplace—jockeying for position, corporate favoritism, and envy—are usually expressions of childhood wishes and the dynamics that went with them. Behind concrete business contracts hide many wishes and expectations that can muddy even clearly defined business interactions. What follows are two illustrations of business contracts that became muddied by wishes.

The Disappointment of a Graphic Designer

Sandra was single, bright, attractive, and a skilled graphic designer. She loved her career and invested a lot of time and energy in it. She prided herself on the clever, creative advertisements she designed, and she was highly respected in her field.

Eight months ago she landed a prized position that almost doubled her salary. She was pleased. Her new boss was also quite pleased. Her employment seemed like a win-win situation. But without realizing it, Sandra began turning it into a win-lose for herself.

She admired her boss a great deal, and it was a pleasure working for him. It was so pleasurable that she often put in overtime. Knowing he could count on her, he always called on Sandra for his special projects. She enjoyed the special status and never said no. He compensated her fairly for her overtime on these extra projects, but it was really his praises and obvious gratitude that kept Sandra working so hard. She didn't even keep track of her work hours. It felt like a labor of love.

So Sandra was working sixty hours a week. When she wasn't at work, she was creating new designs in her mind or figuring out ways to please her boss. The few times she got together with friends or family, she only talked about her work—what a great person her new boss was and how much she enjoyed working for him.

Beginning about the fifth month, however, her attitude toward her job started to sour. She became curt with coworkers. She even became disgruntled with the special tasks her boss gave her. She was less motivated, had difficulty concentrating, and had lost her creative edge.

Obviously, she was burning out. Less obviously, there was an unfulfilled wish driving her to the point of burnout. Sandra was really working under *two* contracts at her job—the *stated* contract that she and her boss had agreed on and signed and an *unstated* contract.

The unstated contract involved unresolved wishes from childhood that she had brought to the job. These wishes grew out of her early interactions with her parents, who had loved her a great deal. But her father had very high standards and was highly critical of her. She had internalized his critical attitude. Spurred on by a harsh, inner taskmaster, she had always worked very hard at whatever she did. She was trying to prove to her father and to herself that she was good enough.

Without meaning to, her boss was stepping right into these father wishes. He acknowledged her good work. He appreciated her. With him, she *was* good enough. In fact, she seemed to perform *beyond* his expectations. She delighted in what felt like a wish come true—at least for the first four months.

But bringing deep-seated father wishes to the work arena also created major problems for Sandra. She felt resentful whenever her boss praised anyone else's work. She wanted to be the star at work and was jealous when anyone shared in the limelight. She became competitive with coworkers in ways that actually hurt the teamwork and left her looking petty. She even became disgruntled with her boss. There was no doubt that he valued her work highly, but he treated her like an employee, not like a daughter.

She was so involved in work that she sacrificed her social life too. She wanted to marry…someday. But right now she had no time to date. Work seemed too important.

Actually, the process of meeting new men had always felt risky to Sandra. Because of her father issues, she was particularly sensitive to being criticized or rejected by men, and she shied away from the whole dating scene. Now work provided a good excuse to sidestep it. Besides, when basking in her boss's praise, it was easy to feel as though she *did* have a special man in her life.

Work also provided a substitute social life of sorts. At first, she had enjoyed interacting with her coworkers. And the interactions felt safer—structured around a task and therefore more predictable—than the free-floating interactions at social get-togethers or singles' mixers.

So Sandra was expecting work to be her whole life—family life, social life, and entertainment. This did not make for a sane perspective at work. Putting so much time and energy into her work inflamed her unrealistic wishes. Because she was sacrificing so much for her work, she expected a lot in return. She felt entitled to specialness and to having these deep-seated wishes fulfilled. The result was that she felt increasingly dissatisfied with her work and with her boss. She became angrier and angrier that she was not getting her due. And she was not even aware of the deep-seated wishes fueling her discontent.

There could be any of several outcomes for Sandra at this point. She could continue putting in many hours with less and less return… and maybe eventually lose her job. Her burnout could develop into a major depression, and she might take a temporary leave from her work on workman's compensation. She could become *so* angry she might try to build a case for a lawsuit against the company. Or she could seek therapy for her obvious symptoms before they got out of hand.

That's what she did. In therapy Sandra began examining what it was she was truly wanting from her job. She began to understand the unrealistic father wishes she was unwittingly expecting her boss to fulfill. And she began to face her father wishes. Over time she felt deeply sad about how intensely she had longed for her father to celebrate her little-girl achievements. First, she felt angry, and then she wept, remembering how much his high standards and criticism had hurt her. She was facing the unmet wishes of childhood, and she was mourning.

As she mourned and let go of these wishes that could never be granted, she was freed from a slavery that had been consuming her life. Gradually, she stopped seeking her father's approval and took charge of her life. She enjoyed her work more than ever—all forty to forty-five hours a week of it! She still appreciated her boss's appreciation of her, but the meaning of it changed for her. It was a boss's appreciation for a job well done—nothing more. It was not worth giving her whole life for. As she put work in its proper perspective, she began to take the risks needed to create a rich and full life for herself.

Disappointment in a Therapist

Brad was seeing a therapist. On one appointment day, he had unexpected demands at work, and he called to cancel his therapy session. Later on, he was surprised to find he had been charged for the session. He had known that his therapist required twenty-four hours for a cancellation to avoid billing. But Brad reasoned he could not help the cancellation. After all, his work was very important. He pointed out the error to his therapist and became irate when she simply reminded him of the twenty-four-hour cancellation policy to which he had agreed. He believed her enforcement of the policy was preposterous and threatened to quit therapy.

This was the fourth therapist Brad had seen in thirteen months. Therapy had always reached a point of impasse when the therapist did something that seemed unreasonable to Brad. He would become terribly angry, leave, and look for someone "more reasonable," someone who could understand him better.

This had been a pattern in Brad's personal relationships as well. It's a great tragedy for any of us to reach thirty or forty or sixty years of age and have a history of broken relationships because we are always leaving in disappointment or anger, always looking for others who will love us more or understand us better.

This is the pattern created by bitterness, by pursuing and demanding fulfillment of unrealistic wishes, and it makes for an empty life. Loneliness is always having the perfect relationship…just around the next corner. This was the story of Brad's life.

A surprising thing happened, however. Brad paused before walking out the door in a rage. That pause was life-changing and was prompted by the awareness of a couple of things on Brad's part. First, Brad realized he had really liked his therapist before the rage episode. Second, he was aware that he didn't like his history of short-term relationships. So this time he paused to try to understand why he was so enraged at the therapist's enforcement of the twenty-four-hour policy—a policy he himself had agreed to.

As Brad and the therapist explored his outburst, he began to understand that underneath it all was a wish for an ideal mother. He began to see how his wish was impeding his long-term friendships.

Brad's mother had been cold and emotionally unavailable. She was a rigid, letter-of-the-law type who thought rules were made to be followed at any cost. When the therapist enforced her twenty-four-hour policy, it tapped into Brad's horror of his mother's legalism—a legalism that had stamped out his personhood as a little boy. For a moment, his therapist seemed just like his inner image of a rigid, depriving mother, and Brad was furious with her.

But even in his fury, he began to have an inkling that the fury wasn't really about his therapist. Ironically, the rage that almost prompted him to quit therapy became the trigger for his first real work in therapy. He traced the rage to its roots—his disappointed longings for a mother who could be warm and spontaneous and simply *enjoy* her little boy. As Brad explored the real meanings of his rage, he began to mourn and to let go of the wishes behind it.

In therapy Brad was able at last to deal constructively with his rage rather than to continue to act it out blindly in his current relationships. Because he was taking responsibility for his rage and longings, he could begin to give up his unrealistic demands of people. He saw how he had taken his unmet childhood longings to his therapist…and to many people before her. He came to understand that nobody (not even his therapist) could go back in time and undo the little-boys hurts. Only he could resolve these past hurts by facing them, feeling them, and working through them. As he accepted responsibility for his past struggles, he became more and more open to taking in the good gifts that friends and loved ones *could* give him. Not surprisingly, among these good gifts were the warmth, spontaneity, and enjoyment for which he had always longed.

CHAPTER 20

THE MANY WISHES OF MOTHERHOOD AND FATHERHOOD

So far we have looked at adults who need to let go of unrealistic wishes springing from childhood losses. But we have not yet looked at the need for adults to let go of wishes related to the task of parenting. Parents are yearning human beings too. The capacity for learning to love our children well is absolutely dependent on a willingness to mourn the loss of the unrealistic wishes we have toward them. These may be wishes for a daughter when parents had to give up trying after the third son, wishes for a child to become a doctor who instead becomes an artist, or wishes for that special parent-child bond that never quite materializes.

Mothers and fathers, with unique yet interweaving contributions to their children's development, have remarkably similar wishes to be mourned. Mothers are a baby's first love. It is the mother who carries the infant in her womb, who breastfeeds the infant, and who establishes that first intimacy with the young baby. But fathers quickly emerge as adored figures in their own right, modeling a strength and presence so important in its own way to the infant's growth and well-being. The sheer unbridled need of infants as well as their ready responsiveness and bonding as simple needs are met—as they are loved—can stir fierce, intense love in both parents. And where there is fierce, intense love there are also fierce, intense wishes. Many of these wishes will come true. Many will not. There will be many frustrated wishes to be mourned before that final mourning we refer to as empty-nest syndrome. These disappointed wishes, which all mothers and fathers experience as children grow up, need to be better understood.

Parents begin wishing when their children are very young. They must become students to their infants, learning the many meanings of their cries and quickly responding to their various needs. At first, mothers and fathers may enjoy a seemingly godlike power to soothe their babies and make everything okay. Their first and most fervent wish becomes the wish to secure goodness and well-being for their children.

But after a while, life becomes more complex. Even as the growing children are embracing opinions, pastimes, and other people that could hurt them, the parents need to begin to relinquish control over their children. They must give up their wishes to manage their children's lives and to oversee their outcomes in ways that would seem to guarantee their happiness. Increasingly, there are times when they must sit back in brooding silence, watching, knowing but unable to intervene and make things work out for their children. When should they intervene actively? When should they trust the children's internalized wisdom? And when should they let them learn through their own experiences?

These are hard and at times agonizing judgment calls that confront both parents. To further complicate things, it may seem that as the children mature, the ground rules are always shifting. Mothers and fathers feel intense wishes toward their children at each stage of development, but as the children mature, it is essential that these wishes be progressively released. Their natural and helpful wishes are appropriate for their children at one minute, and they have outgrown them at the next.

Wishes Triggered in a Mother

Jo had to let go of some wishes. The feelings that her newborn infant Timmy had stirred in her were incredible. She had never thought it possible to love another human being as she loved Timmy. Her love for Timmy was genuine, but in addition, this little guy was triggering intense longings for closeness from Jo's own infancy—longings that had not been met. Now she could help create the magical infancy for her son that she herself had always wanted. Jo cuddled and played with Timmy, thoroughly entranced by him. She truly enjoyed this baby.

This was good for Timmy and good for Jo. Then one day when Timmy was about six months old, Jo began to weep. She could see that Timmy was no longer the helpless infant he had been. The magical infancy was coming to an end. Through her tears she said, "Timmy, you are so precious. You're growing up, and you're going to leave me."

Jo was so right. She was not clinging to or guilt-tripping Timmy. She was simply preparing to mourn the many wishes she would have to release as Timmy grew up.

This need to mourn the loss of wishes as a child matures is a typical pattern in parenting. Just as we adore the infancy of newborns, we need to support their toddling away. Just as we have adjusted to and become intrigued by their toddling little forays into the world about them, we need to leave them at the door of kindergarten. And just as we've given up being the cherished center of their world to share them with also cherished teachers, they become absorbed in the adolescent world of peers.

The wishes of parenthood are particularly painful and poignant because as mothers or fathers enter fully into parenting, they will see their own childhood replayed before them. Each stage of development their child encounters will trigger unresolved issues from that same stage in the parents' experiences. The infant before them may well bring up many ungratified longings and yearnings from their childhood. If they have not had a good launch themselves, parenting can be a harrowing task. Parents may feel they are having their noses rubbed in all the unfulfilled wishes and unresolved losses from which they have fled in the past.

To further complicate matters, because of these unresolved past issues, parents at times may feel deeply depressed, unresponsive, or irritated with their children. They may torment themselves for having negative feelings toward the children whom they love. They do not realize the child is simply tapping into unresolved hurts from *their* childhood.

These unresolved issues from our past thwart still another fervent wish of parenthood. We wish we could raise our children differently from the way we were raised. We wish we could learn from the mistakes of our own pasts and not repeat them. We *never* want to hurt our children in the ways we were hurt.

Sometimes we are able to improve upon our own parents' parenting, but sometimes it seems as though we cannot. Instead we reflexively play out our hurts and flaws in ways that hurt our children. We see ourselves reenacting with our child scenes from our own childhood we swore we would never repeat.

A Mother's Wish to Be Ideal

Having grown up under an irritable mother and a demeaning father, Maria had sworn her little girl would not be raised in a similar circumstance. But she was unable to deliver many of her ideals and even some of the *just basics* she had dreamed for her little girl.

Maria's husband had divorced her, and she agonized as she watched Teresa struggle to maintain her girlish self-esteem (that special feminine sense of desirability as a woman) without a father to adore her steadily. She winced when Teresa said she missed "mommy hugs" after school when Maria was busy earning a living for the single-parent household. And she hated her own grouchiness when she was home with Teresa but too exhausted to do a good job of mothering.

There are few things harder than seeing ourselves mired in our own childhood hurts and acting them out upon our children. We do it, and we hate it, but we do not know how to stop it. Not in the moment.

Maria felt this kind of deep anguish over the real deficits in her mothering. She made a decision to let her anguish motivate her toward a course of personal growth. But growth would take time. Meanwhile, knowing her own limitations, she made sure that Teresa had other parent figures in her life in addition to Maria herself. This is probably mothering at its best: We have the humility to realize we're not ideal. We deeply regret our mistakes even as we make them. We struggle to improve. And we ask for help from other people who can fill in our deficits.

There is no perfection. Probably the best thing parents have to offer their children is a willingness to grow up *with* the children and to be quick to say, "I'm sorry." As parents, we simply need willingly to accept responsibility for our own flaws and struggle to outgrow them. It doesn't come naturally. We have to really work at change. In the face of repeated mistakes, we can only explain to the child, "I'm so sorry. That was not your fault. It was my fault." Then we need to listen for how the child was hurt by our mistake, and we need to comfort this hurt.

This is doubly hard if we are tormented by feelings of inadequacy, incompetence, or badness when we have hurt our children. But it is important to deal with our feelings of inadequacy or badness on our own time and with our own friends. Then we can let our children express their hurts and anger to us rather than needing them to reassure us that we are good parents.

This need to let our children confront us with our mistakes suggests we must be willing to face yet another lost wish—the wish to be ideal parents. (This is a wish for an ideal self.) Winnicott, a wise pediatrician and psychoanalyst, once emphasized that there is no perfect mother, only "good enough" mothers.[1] (The same can be said of fathers.) Trying to be perfect introduces another whole set of errors in child-rearing. Being alert to our own mistakes, being willing to grow slowly if somewhat painfully, and being willing to apologize in honest ways that allow our children to express their hurt—along with steadily giving all the love we can muster—is "good enough" mothering and fathering. It is parenting at its best.

There's No More Difficult Task

In his deeply moving allegory, *A Symphony in Sand*, Calvin Miller aptly portrays the pathos of the disappointed wishes of motherhood in an analogy to Mary's loss suffered at Jesus's crucifixion.

In the story a woman named Trouvere wanders sleepless through the night. She encounters a weeping woman huddled by a wall along the way. Trouvere asks the woman why she is weeping. The woman explains that she just came from the city where she witnessed the death of her son.

> "My only son was executed there,
> And I beheld him die," The woman said.
> "Have you children?" The huddled being asked
> The question muffled by her buried face.[2]

Then the weeping woman goes on, reflecting on her first tender moments with her son after his birth:

> "I held him close and loved him for his helplessness
> and need.
> That memory shall never leave
> For today I watched him die.
> No man can die a man

While any mother's there to see.
He died a little boy! A child who needed me!
And hurting were his eyes
As when he was a boy!

"He spoke but one word, 'Mother.'
His was not a man's voice,
Nor was his pain a man's pain.
He was a boy crying out to me,
Somehow as he did
When once he scraped a knee or
Felt a fishhook tear his infant hand.
I knew what to do back then.
Today I did not know."[3]

Then the weeping woman relates her final parting with her son.

"I held his wounded head a final time
And wept and said, 'O son!
Think not this furious turn of circumstance
Could ever turn me from the obligations of my
motherhood.
I held you when you took your first, new breath.
I hold you now beyond all final need of breath.'
I kissed him then and called him 'sonny.'
It was not his name
And yet the name I'd always called him
When he fell asleep on my lap.
'Sleep, sonny, for this world did not deserve your
presence.'"[4]

Then Trouvere reached out to lift up the weeping woman's face toward her own so that she could see her, and she made a startling discovery:

The faces were identical!
The woman was herself! [5]

At some point in the task of mothering, each of us must discover this weeping woman in ourselves. The weeping woman is the woman who must give up speaking and silently watch her growing children make their own choices (and mistakes) while always struggling to discern how she might be helpful to the emerging adults. She is the one who learns the difference between the time to embrace and the time to refrain from embracing, between the time to gather up and the time to let go, between the time to speak and the time to remain silent (see Eccl 3). And she is the one who gives up her fervent wish to protect the infants and the growing children from all harm in order to release the maturing young men and women to a world from which she cannot protect them. Silently, the weeping woman prays and trusts that the wisdom and love that she has imparted will continue to guide her children in their choices along their ways.

There is probably no more poignant or difficult task of mourning than the task that mothers encounter in letting go of their fervent wishes toward their growing children.

This call to weep applies equally to men. Fathers also, loving their children deeply, will need to mourn profound lost wishes in the service of loving and letting their children's real personhood emerge.

A Father's Wish to Protect His Little Girl

Sam was a tough, wiry man, slight in build but imposing in presence. Raised in a rough urban environment, he exuded an unmistakable *don't mess with me* vibe…which his daughter Danielle had melted through right from birth. Protecting her from all harm quickly became the most compelling wish of his life. He loved her dearly and deeply.

He also loved his wife, Desiree, dearly and deeply. They shared a robust, very real love and respect for each other born of rich shared experiences—a toughness that came of fighting their way out of poor neighborhoods; a huge capacity for hard work; street smarts that readily sensed phonies and danger; and an unflinching optimism that they could create a better life for their family.

Trading in rough urban life for suburbia, Sam was satisfied that he was fulfilling his wish to secure safety for his family. But he didn't realize that he carried the rough urban neighborhood with him in the form of deeply internalized traumatic memories.

Sam had suffered trauma as a boy. It was not the trauma of parental abuse. His single-parent mother loved and protected him fiercely, determined that he would have the very outcomes he'd achieved in adulthood: a solid education, a rewarding career, and a sweet family.

Rather, it was the trauma of frequent, random violence in his neighborhood—violence which was unpredictable, out of control, terrifying, and shattering in its impact on Sam as a little boy.

Sam made it a point not to think about the violence. But unresolved memories of the violence, cowering out of awareness in unconscious memory, left Sam reactive to unexpected noise and movement. In a modest household of three, one of them being a small, exuberant child, there were lots of unexpected noise and movement. Sam worked hard to contain his reactions but couldn't always do it. There were times he lost his temper badly.

It wasn't primarily anger at play in his temper. It was terror which then triggered an instant rage. The adrenaline of the rage left him feeling powerful, safe, and in charge...unlike the little boy who had felt so helplessly endangered before the repeated, unpredictable, vicious assaults of his boyhood.

Thankfully, he never got physical. But Desiree had grown up in a household where angry outbursts meant slapping and beating were soon to come. She couldn't cope with Sam's angry outbursts which triggered terrifying memories from her own childhood. Images of a cruel, raging, and abusive father began to cloud and confuse her love for Sam.

Therapy could have helped this committed, caring couple. But they'd been raised to believe that therapy was for the *worried well* and rich. It was a soft luxury they understandably disdained. "Be tough and push through" was the formula they'd been taught.

So they tried to push through. But they couldn't push through the repetitive rage of unresolved trauma, and Desiree filed for divorce.

Sam was heartbroken over the loss of his family. Both he and Desiree came from broken homes and shared a deep-seated wish not to replicate that heart-wrenching experience for their daughter. But they were repeating the cycle, and both were even more heartbroken at Danielle's heartbreak than at their own.

Danielle didn't like her father's anger, but she knew with certainty that she was loved and prized by both parents. An only child, she felt her whole world crumble as she saw the only other people in her most intimate community abandon their precious family of three. Sam had been so determined to use his strength *always* to protect his daughter. He felt an anguish beyond what he thought possible as he faced his helplessness to rescue Danielle from these unbearable sadnesses—first of his uncontrolled anger and now of the breakup of their family.

In his deep anguish, Sam was mourning the loss of the deepest wishes of his adulthood. He had done everything he knew to protect Danielle from the demons out there in the world, the demons he knew so well…the shattered glass and shattered lives of drive-by shootings; brandished knives and guns, at times hitting their mark; violence against women that left him feeling guilty for being a man even as a little boy; gangs; prostitution. And he *had* protected Danielle from all of these.

But he had not been able to protect her from the demons inside, from his inner world—those haunting memories of trauma capable of evoking in him such knee-jerk emotion—the strong, uncontrollable terror and rage. He had wished with such intensity to protect Danielle from all harm, but he couldn't. Sam was facing devastated wishes and despair. But it was the devastated wishes and despair that prompted him to do something he thought he would *never* do. He faced his limitations and reached out for help.

The effects of trauma are treatable. In therapy, Sam learned how to have compassion on the little boy who had suffered so many scenes of overwhelming violence. He learned how to notice the first sensations in his body that could cue him that he was about to be overwhelmed by terror and rage. He learned how to use these cues to guide him to carry out an action plan designed to prevent a rage episode. He learned to give his body 20 minutes to defuse when terror and rage were about to be triggered. He learned how to negotiate unexpected noise and movement with Desiree and Danielle—who welcomed him back with open arms. He learned how to let love—not trauma—have the last word in his treasured family of three. And he learned how to fulfill his wishes to protect his little girl from every harm, even the demons within.

Biblical Portrayals of the Weeping Man

There are poignant biblical portrayals of this weeping man as well. We see the weeping man in Jesus, weeping over his tender, aching desire to gather the people of Jerusalem under his arms but yielding to their refusal (see Mt 23:37). We see him in Joseph, weeping through so many devastated wishes to once again embrace the brothers who ruthlessly had sold him into slavery (see Gn 42:24; 43:30; 45:1, 2). And one can well imagine the weeping done by that familiar parabolic figure, the father of the prodigal son, who had so many wishes to mourn in order to keep alive his love for his son who would one day return, a changed man (see Lk 15:11-31). Finally, we may sense this weeping man in God the Father watching, perhaps "with groanings too deep for words" (Rom 8:26), as his Son agonizes in Gethsemane (see Mt 26:36-46), endures the torture of crucifixion (see Mt 27:31-50), and, perhaps most painfully, cries out on the cross, "MY GOD, MY GOD, WHY HAST THOU FORSAKEN ME?"

(Mt 27:46). He may well have mourned deeply as he restrained himself from cutting short the suffering of his well-loved Son even as he felt the unspeakable joy of the great salvation being accomplished on our behalf. What an immense sacrificing of wishes toward an ultimate wish that we human beings—mortal, weak, errant, and yet loved—might be ushered into our Father's kingdom and into his very family.

* * *

I conclude this section with a chapter on parenting because mothering and fathering illustrate perhaps better than any other life calling the many wishes that must be relinquished in the service of love. It is offered to comfort mothers and fathers in their very difficult task of launching other human beings. It is also offered to help adult children better understand the dilemma of their parents.

If we understand the hardships of parenting, we may be able to better embrace our mothers and fathers for the people they really are and were. Embracing our parents leads to increased wholeness and joy. When God said, "Honor your mother and father…that it may be well with you" (Eph 6:2, 3), he was not giving us just a difficult spiritual exercise. He was letting us in on a secret of souls and how they become whole.

ENDNOTES

Chapter 1
The Lost Art of Wishing

1   Jan Swafford, *The Vintage Guide to Classical Music* (New York: Random House, Vintage Books, 1992).

Chapter 2
The Child's World of Wishing

1   R. Laird Harris, Gleason L. Archer Jr., and Bruce K. Waltke, eds., *Theological Wordbook of the Old Testament*, vol. 2 (Chicago: Moody, 1992), 587–90.

2   Ronald E. Clements, *Wisdom in Theology* (Grand Rapids, MI: Eerdmans, 1992), 139.

3   Shel Silverstein, *The Missing Piece* (New York: Harper Collins, 1976).

Chapter 3
The Adult's World of Wishing

1   M. Scott Peck, *The Road Less Traveled: A New Psychology of Love, Traditional Values, and Spiritual Growth* (New York: Simon and Schuster, 1978), 15.

2   Judith Viorst, *Necessary Losses: The Loves, Illusions, Dependencies and Impossible Expectations that All of Us Have to Give Up in Order to Grow* (New York: Simon and Schuster, 1986).

3   Rabbi Levi Meier, *Ancient Secrets: Using the Stories of the Bible to Improve Our Everyday Lives* (New York: Random House, Villard, 1996), 104.
4   Colin Brown, ed., *The New International Dictionary of New Testament Theology* (Grand Rapids, MI: Zondervan, 1986), 361–67.

Chapter 5
Defensive Wishing—Part 2: Spoiling

1   Melanie Klein, *Envy and Gratitude & Other Works 1946–1963* (New York: Delacorte, 1975), 181.

Chapter 6
Defensive Wishing—Part 3: Wishing for the Ideal

1   Stephen King, *Needful Things* (New York: Penguin, 1992).

Chapter 7
Depression: The Chronic Mourning of Unrealistic Wishes

1   Adapted from Sigmund Freud, "Mourning and Melancholia," in Willard Gaylin, ed., *Psychodynamic Understanding of Depression* (New York: Jason Aronson, 1983), 51.
2   Sheldon Vanauken, *A Severe Mercy* (San Francisco: Harper San Francisco, 1977, 1980), 180.
3   Vanauken, *A Severe Mercy,* 180.

Chapter 8
Bitterness: A Reservoir of Anger over
Wishes that Haven't Come True

1   C. S. Lewis, *The Screwtape Letters* (New York: Mentor, 1988), 82.

Chapter 9
Shame and Our Disappointed Wishes to Be Ideal

1   Henri J. M. Nouwen, *Life of the Beloved: Spiritual Living in a Secular World* (New York: Crossroad, 1995).

2   Henry Cloud, *Changes that Heal* (Grand Rapids, MI: Zondervan, 1994).

3   G. K. Chesterton, *Orthodoxy: The Romance of Faith* (New York: Image, Doubleday, 1959), 50.

4   Adapted from Karen Horney, *Neurosis and Human Growth: The Struggle Toward Self-Realization* (New York: W. W. Norton, 1991).

5   Leon Wurmser, "Shame: The Veiled Companion of Narcissism," in Donald L. Nathanson, ed., *The Many Faces of Shame* (New York: Guilford, 1987), 80.

Chapter 10
Joy in the Mourning

1   C. S. Lewis, *The Great Divorce* (New York: MacMillan, 1974), 21.

2   Lewis, *The Great Divorce,* 21.

3   Lewis, *The Great Divorce,* 22.

4   Lewis, *The Great Divorce,* 22.

5   Lewis, *The Great Divorce,* 42.

6   Lewis, *The Great Divorce,* 31.

7   C. S. Lewis Foundation, founded by Dr. J. Stanley Matson, PO Box 8008, Redlands, CA 92375, 1-888-CSLEWIS.

Chapter 12
The End of Shame: Letting Go of the Wish for an Ideal Self

1   Alan W. Jones, *Soul Making: The Desert Way of Spirituality* (San Francisco: Harper San Francisco, 1989), 82.

2   Dallas Willard, *Life without Lack: Living in the Fullness of Psalm 23* (Nashville, TN: Nelson Books, 2018).

3   George Ritchie with Elizabeth Sherrill, *Return from Tomorrow* (Tarrytown, NY: Revell, 1978), 54.

Chapter 14
Resolving Bitterness—Part 2: Giving up the Wished for Parent

1   C. S. Lewis, *The Lion, the Witch, and the Wardrobe* (New York: Collier, 1973).

Chapter 16
The Story of Job, and Giving Up Our Wishes for Security

1   Blaise Pascal, *Pensees*, trans. A. J. Krailsheimer (London: Penguin, 1966), 92.
2   Mary Ann Spencer Pulaski, *Understanding Piaget: An Introduction to Children's Cognitive Development* (New York: Harper & Row, 1971).
3   Cooper Edens, *If You're Afraid of the Dark, Remember the Night Rainbow* (New York: Green Tiger, Simon and Schuster, 1979).
4   George MacDonald, *Discovering the Character of God* (Minneapolis: Bethany House, 1989), 77.

Chapter 18
Tragic Choices behind Victimization

1   Malcolm Muggeridge, *Chronicles of Wasted Time* (Washington, DC: Regnery Gateway, 1972, 1973), 274.
2   Pinkola Estes, *Women Who Run With the Wolves* (New York: Ballantine, 1992), 51.
3   Calvin Miller, *A Symphony in Sand* (Dallas: Word, 1990), 83.

Chapter 20
The Many Wishes of Motherhood and Fatherhood

1   D. W. Winnicott, *The Maturational Processes and the Facilitating Environment: Studies in the Theory of Emotional Development* (Madison, CT: International Universities Press, 1991), 145–46.

2   Calvin Miller, *A Symphony in Sand,* 86.

3   Miller, *A Symphony in Sand,* 87.

4   Miller, *A Symphony in Sand,* 89.

5   Miller, *A Symphony in Sand,* 89.

CPSIA information can be obtained
at www.ICGtesting.com
Printed in the USA
BVHW031405060619
550362BV00008B/354/P

9 781973 659761